MAGICKAL MUSINGS OF A ROGUE WITCH

CHERYL COSTA

SKY GODDESS PRESS
an imprint of
DRAGON LADY MEDIA, LLC
ROCKY RIVER, OHIO
2022

First edition 2022
ISBN: 9798408549207

Cover design by Cheryl Costa
Cover Photo: Jackie Vidler - Enfoqué Images
https://www.enfoqueimages.com/
Carol Hollenbeck - Editor
Linda Miller Costa – Editor & Publisher
Printed & Distributed by Amazon.com

Publisher:
SKY GODDESS PRESS an imprint of
Dragon Lady Media, LLC
Rocky River, Ohio
skygoddessevents@gmail.com

DEDICATION

To all the Witches, Mages, Mystics and Adepts, who wrote the books that gave me pieces of greater knowledge.

To all the Magickal and Mystical mentors of my life. Your wisdom, insights, and heartfelt advice guided my path.

To my hundreds of Wicca and Magickal students. Your questions were exit signs on the road to greater understanding.

To the Lamas of the Tibetan Orthodox Tradition, who taught me to tame my mind and listen to the song of the Great Consciousness.

To All Magickal Adepts, Past, Present and Future
and most especially to my favorite hedge witch!

Contents

Preface

I began my study in the mystical and magickal arts in the fall of 1976, while in the Navy. Since that time, I have embraced the moniker of "Witch." Around 2004, I also began embracing the epithet of "Mystic" as well. These days I might refer to myself as a Mystic Witch. Why do I make this distinction? Because I approached my craft from the view of practicing what had been taught to me from books and living teachers. But I also approached my craft from a perspective of exploration. This led to mentoring by magickal elders in a wide range of traditions and even led to me spending seven years in Buddhist monastic life, therefore attaining a wider Mystical view.

When I started in the Craft, I was dependent on the scant published materials about witchcraft practices that I had managed to accumulate. In effect, all my practices were simply parroting what other people had done. Like just about everybody else, I started out with simple spell casting which seemed to be the normal path to the Witchcraft arts. Spell casting, from my view, amounted to nothing more than practicing other people's recipes.

In the early 1980s I became acquaintances with a seasoned Ceremonial Magician. She explained to me that of some fifty magick related books on her shelf, she had distilled down from perhaps ten of her books the magickal techniques that worked for her. Were her other books useless? No, not really but she did point out that some of those authors were simply echoing what others had said. She instilled in me the golden rule of "test everything, keep the techniques that work, and do your best to discover new things."

This book is not a textbook! This book is just what it's entitled to be, it's my Musings about Magick. Think of the individual essays as the conversations I might have shared with you over tea and scones at our favorite café.

Since my highly evolved approach to mysticism and magickal practices is presented in a shop talk style, I suggest that you approach the enclosed material with the heart of a beginner.

Some of the essays within were originally written for my former column in Wicca Magazine. Other essays were exclusively written for my final class of students during the Pandemic year of 2020, when I was forced to teach virtually.

When a priestess retires from public pastoral duties, there is an expectation that the witch will write a book about their long view on the magickal and mystical arts. Some publish a recipe book of all their best spells. Others publish writings on how to start and manage covens and other forms of magickally related groups.

In Magick INTENTION is everything! I have chosen to publish my understanding of magickal mysticism in terms of the elementary building blocks of magickal mechanics in a plain English disclosure style. I hope you will enjoy this book as the mystical primer it was intended to be.

What is a Rogue Witch

When the publisher of this manuscript and I were trying to name the book, we went through a number of variations.

We considered "The Magickal Ravings of a Mad Priestess" but we discarded this because it suggested that I was insane.

We also considered "The Magickal Musings of a Mad Crone" again we discarded it for suggesting that I was upset or deranged.

After much consideration and lively discussion, we settled on **"The Magickal Musings of a Rogue Witch."** The reason being that for many years, no decades, I have not been a follower. Many people have pointed out that I always cut my own path.

The Merriam-Webster online dictionary in its adjective definition of **Rogue** asserts:

go rogue: *to begin to behave in an independent or uncontrolled way that is not authorized, normal, or expected*

> Definition Attribution: Dictionary by Merriam-Webster: America's most-trusted online dictionary. https://www.merriam-webster.com/

I started out as a Solitary Witchcraft practitioner like most witches. Realistically each Solitary practitioner usually starts with some reading and experimentation. Slowly over many years and yes, decades, a Solitary hones their personal practice to suit themselves. A magickal adept's practice will most assuredly evolve over the years. Most adepts that I've known are seriously utilitarian, using what works for them and discarding what doesn't work or what doesn't apply to the way they practice. First and foremost, all magickal adepts are basically Solitaries! We all have our own solitary way of doing things.

Let us also dispel the other popular Hollywood notion, that all magickal adepts are members of Covens. Nope, not by a long shot! As I previously stated all magickal adept practitioners are fundamentally solitaries, so I am not alone in the Rogue definition.

Sometimes loose groups of solitaries known to each other get together for pot-luck dinners, celebrations, and spiritual fellowship. I call these gatherings **Gaggles.** Then there might be a slightly more organized, more regular and positively more focused group, we might call that a **Circle**. Over the years I have been a participant in many circles and even founded a few. Mostly because I wanted more magickal friends to hang out with.

Finally, there are **Covens**, they are rarer. Covens are tight, somewhat exclusive and usually by invitation only. Why so private? Think of a coven as a well-practiced performance drill team. All the members of a coven are on the same page, rehearsed and holding the focus of the Coven's objectives clearly as a point of single-mindedness.

Have I ever been a member of a bonafide Coven? Nope.

While five or six covenants over forty years have invited and considered me, I was deemed to be too much of a ***wild duck*** for their tastes and temperament. My spontaneous nature was not in affinity with the greater group.

Was this a bad thing that I was not installed as a member in those groups? A coven leader many years later told me that my talents had been better utilized along another path.

But for me **Rogue** goes a great deal deeper. In 1991, I began producing a cable television program about American Witchcraft. I had hoped to be the host but there was push back because I was a transwoman and in 1991 the elders and many others who heard of what I was going to produce "Didn't want a transsexual Priestess representing the magickal community on television!"

Considering that I needed the general support of the regional magickal community at large as guests for the program, I conceded to this mandate. A close friend, 25-year-old Kestryl Angell stepped up and became the face of Witchcraft on my program. I stayed behind the scenes and ran things as the Executive Producer. Initially, the program only had a contract for six measly episodes so the senior magickal community was content that the program would be short lived and the risk that I would be in the spotlight was considered minimal.

A week before the program was supposed to air, an Associated Press wire story was filed, and suddenly massive amounts of mainstream media attention began raining down on that tiny Virginia Cable station. And literally overnight Kestryl and I became the flavor of the week in the media news cycle, as publicly out and in your face Witches!

About half of the mid-Atlantic magickal community accepted what was happening as a good thing and the other half grumbled and did their best behind the scenes to squash magickal community support for the program. Nevertheless, I, Kestryl, and my production team received additional follow-on production contracts and we produced some seventy half hour episodes over two years, and we were the subject of some 90 plus domestic and international media stories.

Back in 1991-1992, cable systems in smaller communities had perhaps 7-10 channels. In larger metropolitan areas the cable systems had perhaps 20-25 channels. But nationally new cable networks with new and specialized programs were starting to blossom. A couple of months before Kestryl announced that she was leaving, one of these new fledgling networks approached me about taking the "Kestryl and Company" program "national."

Afterall, we had produced 70 high quality programs with a shoestring budget in a local market, and we enjoyed nearly 100 domestic and international media interviews in print, radio and television. As one national journalist commented a short while later. *"What do these two kitchen witches know that the moguls in Hollywood don't? Perhaps they really do know Magic!"*

But after two years of being the face of Witchcraft on cable, Kestryl was burned out and wanted to leave the program. I had filled in as host for Kestryl for a couple of episodes when she wasn't available. So, when Kestryl was getting ready to leave, the cable station and the representatives for the national network wanted me to become the new host.

That's when I started getting unpleasant phone calls from representatives of influential Craft families and pagan groups and others that didn't want me-a transsexual woman-to be the Face of Witchcraft. As leverage, they were in a position to shut off my supply of regional guests. Faced with having a local/national program with no local source of guests. I shut down and walked away.

In 1994, I became a fan regular on a silly mainstream afternoon radio program. My on-air name was Lady Cassandra, and I made no bones about being a card-carrying witch and a transsexual woman. The two professional radio hosts had lots of fun with it.

Of course, my occasional high visibility presence on a #1 rated comedic radio program that was nationally syndicated gave those aforementioned prominent Craft families and pagan groups serious heart burn. To be honest with you they wanted me to go crawl under a rock and NOT come out.

In 1995, several of us fan regulars went off and started our own radio program on a small AM radio station. The premise of the program was rowdy women's locker room talk on Saturday night. The two principle hosts were Francis a big breasted Blonde bombshell, and me Cassandra. I was billed as the Bionic trans-woman and a witch. The program was very funny! Despite the fact we were on a dinky AM station, our exotic mystique and unique comedy began drawing press, magazine and television visibility. As one station manager at a major DC station was later quoted, *"Those women and that little AM station have garnered more press in two years than most stations accumulate in ten."*

In December 1997, we were invited to be the Christmas break replacement for the Morning Show 6am-9am on a fifty-thousand-watt AM station in the Washington, DC market. For a week we rocked the morning AM radio market. On the last program of that week the General Manager informed the audience that the station was picking us up and we would be on Saturday-nights. Nearly a year later in the fall of 1998, the marketing people came to the rest of the cast to ask them to minimize my visibility. They had complaints about me being a Trans-woman and a witch to boot. I left the program, and I might add "took my magick with me."

I was picked up two weeks later by the dinky AM station the rowdy gals radio program started on. This was a solo gig as an anchor talk host and the topic matter was Paranormal, the Metaphysical, and Anomalous stuff. Naturally, I was a good fit. The program was called "The X Factor."

The Rogue Witch was at it again and my source of guests this time were authors of the wild and weird stuff and every flavor of the metaphysical. Several publishers sent me a regular stream of guests and my weekly two-hour program quickly became the media outlet in the Washington, DC market to visit if you had a book on off the wall topics. Of course, the mid-Atlantic magickal Cabal saw to it that no local metaphysical guests would appear on my radio program. So be it. I did the weekly program from December 1998 through April 2001.

I took a hiatus from media for dozen years. At this point I was retired from my professional aerospace system engineering job, and I was finishing a long overdue bachelor's degree in entertainment writing with the State University of New York.

In 2013 I began pitching newspaper editors in upstate New York and proposed a weekly column about the topic of Unidentified Flying Objects (UFOs). The Syracuse New Times, a small weekly newspaper hired me as a free-lance columnist. The UFO column was an immediate hit, and I wrote it for the newspaper, for seven years until they went out of business in 2019.

In 2018 thru 2020, I produced and hosted a talk radio program on a Las Vegas radio station called "Cosmic Questions." The program was pure magick and witchcraft topic matter.

As of this writing in the fall of 2021, I am slated to launch another Mystical and Magickal venue in a global online streaming program in early 2022 with a UK outfit, called Zykotika on a YouTube Channel. It's going to be Mystical talk and Magick made easy. This program will be about Magickal Disclosure, in other words, putting the mechanics of magick out there for all to partake!

Nobody from the old Witchcraft cabal has spoken up and I doubt they will. They couldn't control me in the 1990s, they most certainly aren't going to sit on me in 2022.

I am a talented magickal practitioner and an OUT and in-your-face **Rogue Witch**!

I plow my own field and plant the seeds of magickal knowledge and wisdom everywhere I go!

"Let there be magick for all who can master it." SO, MOTE IT BE!

Part One -What Magical Practice Really Is

Magick - The Art of Bending Reality

Consider for a moment the idea that reality is pliable and bendable. Furthermore, consider that real life mystics have been massaging reality's pliable points using metaphysical techniques for millennia.

Magic is a topic that fascinates us!

Stage magic dazzles and entertains us. But Stage magic, as you know, is cleverness and the art of illusion.

Of course, there are the high-tech Computer-Generated Images (CGI) that we see in modern motion pictures, the proverbial movie magic.

Then there is the magic that we read about in fairytales. It's powerful magic usually wielded by sorcerers and the ever-present stereotype witch. Magic in storybooks is made real by the powerful prose and most certainly our own imaginations. It is in essence theater-of-the-mind.

Then there is a real-life Magick. Please note the variant spelling with a "K" that magickal adepts use to denote the art of the reality-bending practice.

Of course, most people will tell you that magick is simply make-believe. They will assure you that such things do not exist. There are a few people who believe in the power of magick. Usually, these are not people who practice magick, nor do they really understand a thing about it. They are happy to bend your ear and tell you that magick is dangerous and not to be fooled around with. They also frequently say those who practice magick are evil. There are also many people who believe that only a divine being can manifest genuine magick.

Still others are skeptical, but they leave the door open for real magick. Unfortunately, they frequently expect real-world practitioners to perform abundant and mighty feats. They almost always want over-the-top and overt demonstrations. Yet many of these people are less than impressed when a genuine practitioner demonstrates some small feat that defies the laws of physics. *"It's not good enough,"* they say. In fact, it's never good enough for them. They almost always label it a parlor trick or call it a coincidence.

The truth of the matter is that Reality is a construct; therefore, it is bendable and malleable. I once read a passage in a book by Buddhist Scholar Robert Thurman where he described that experienced lamas are literally immersed in the art of manipulating the "machine code" of reality. Magickal adepts have been doing this sort of thing to one degree or another for millennia.

Buddhist and Magickal practitioners alike understand that there is a Great Common Consciousness, which we magickal adepts call the Higher Self. We also both understand the idea of the dualist view. An adept refers to our personal aspect of the great consciousness as the Younger Self and our day-to-day human perspective as the Talking Self.

The basic technique of magick is simple enough in theory. It only requires communicating our intention from our Talking Self to the Younger Self to the Great Consciousness (Higher Self) for manifestation. That sounds like a "prayer" doesn't it? In effect, it is a prayer of sorts.

Bottom line, all efforts to manifest something through supernatural means works through this mechanism. Some might call the Great Consciousness by a God or Goddess name or by perhaps a Buddhist Bodhisattva name. Folks grounded in Star Wars mythos might call it The Force.

By whatever name you call it, the principle is still the same; ultimately, we are merely trying to get our intention communicated to the Higher Self or Great Consciousness to manifest the causes to turn our thought into form.

This metaphysical communication also works in another way, the gathering of information which some call Divining. As a Buddhist lama once told me, meditate on it and be open to the knowledge. So instead of experiencing something to know it, you contemplate it and come to know it without experiencing.

A student asked a Zen teacher how he should learn a particular thing. The teacher simply told the student to "know it." This is the gaining of knowledge without experiencing it; this too can be accomplished by touching the Great Consciousness. This is the technique that military Remote Viewers used to gather intelligence information through psychic means.

In the movies, we are shown that great sorcerers read aloud powerful spells from venerable ancient books of magic. Such a scene makes for high drama but falls short in terms of actual magickal technique.

As a mystic, I will take three old ladies focused on saying a rosary, versus a supposed great sorcerer reading a long-winded, verbose spell, any time. Why?

Communication to the younger self is on a more primal level. Verbose higher language doesn't cut it! To communicate with the younger self, you need to use art like symbols, play acting, music, and dancing. Think of magickal practice as a non-verbal game like charades.

For example, you want to have a new bicycle manifest in your life. An excellent simple technique is to cut out a lot of photos of the bike you want and stick them up on your mirror, your doors, and even the wall across from your toilet seat. Put the pictures up any place where you can observe the photo in a relaxed state of mind. The other approach would be to engage those three old ladies with the rosary beads. Why?

The reciting of prayers is known as a mantra. Repetition of mantra is a time-honored technique for quieting-the-mind. So now we reach the heart of the matter, quieting-the-mind.

Whether we are trying to divine or remote view information from the Great Consciousness-Higher Self or trying to impress a magickal request for the manifestation of something, in reality, the key to both scenarios is quieting-the-mind.

Other time-honored methods for quieting-the-mind are chanting, drumming and ceremonial dancing. Meditation is an excellent way to do what all the different techniques eventually achieve, mental quieting.

The process of quieting the "monkey chatter" in your mind makes it possible to non-verbally communicate an intention from the younger self to the higher self.

If you decide to learn meditation and perhaps the arts of magick, I caution you that to start any of it requires that you shut your phone off during your efforts.

Quieting the mind is the primary requirement for working magick. The quieter the mind, the crisper the non-verbal imagery required for first-rate manifestation. Experienced magickal adepts understand that quieting the monkey mind chatter is what it is all about!

A couple of last thoughts, Magick isn't hard, and it isn't easy either. Practicing the art of magick requires training, focus, practice discipline and a flexibility to adapt.

A wise person does not dabble at magick! True Magickal Adepts make a heartfelt life's commitment to the art. Real Magickal Adepts learn that Magick is an **Art**, a **Science** and a **Lifestyle**.

Art, Science and a Lifestyle

Magickal practice is an **Art**. If practiced regularly and with a degree of spontaneity it is most certainly an **Art**. As with any art there are issues of developed skill and technique.

Many magickal adepts find that they never practice magick the same way twice. First, it's difficult to repeat certain physical and mental actions the same way multiple times. Oh yes, we can rehearse something but the activity of rehearsing something, in fact, changes- you the practitioner. So, because you are now changed the whole situation of the spontaneous ritualistic activity is different.

As with any performance art there is always a degree of spontaneous improvisation. All artists do it. That's why it's called an artistic practice.

> **Example:** I've been deeply involved in community theater since I was 15. I know from experience that while I can deliver certain dialog lines exactly as written, I know that my mannerism might be slightly different each time I perform the scene. Likewise, I also know my vocal nuances may be a little different with each performance.

> **Example:** My magickal students routinely learn to make bread as an exercise in process discipline. The lesson these students all learn is that two loaves of bread never turn out exactly the same. Because there are multiple variables that are beyond the control of the bread maker.

Magick as a **Science** is a concept that confounds critics and debunkers alike. At issue is the fact that in theory all scientific experiments are repeatable. That is generally true. But over the years I've observed both in college and in industry that supposedly repeatable experiments failed. Why?

Answer: Subtle issues of temperature with the materials being used or perhaps the age of the chemical being used. Sometimes it boils down to the approach of the person conducting the experiment.

> **Example:** All my students learn to make and master a simple loaf of white bread. To begin with they are all given a list of ingredients. They are told what brand to purchase and from what vendor. Likewise, they are told to purchase tools used to measure the temperatures of the oven and the warm water used to wake up the yeast. They are told how many times to knead the dough and how long to let it rise between kneadings. Finally, they must bake the bread in an oven at a certain temperature for a prescribed period of time. The initial results among 12-15 students range from a golden perfectly formed loaf to a series of malformed loaves and finally some out and out disasters. Analysis of each loaf typically finds either a materials issues like the wrong kind of flour, sugar or yeast. Likewise, some people thought they could take short cuts in the overall process of making the bread. Some were sloppy about it and didn't properly measure ingredients or confirm the proper baking temperature or didn't pay attention to the critical temperature of the water used with the yeast. Too cold and the yeasts

won't wake up, too hot and you'll kill the yeasts. So much for the repeatable experiment.

Magick as a **Lifestyle.** Magickal thinking and practices most assuredly will change your lifestyle. That said, the knee jerk reaction I usually hear after I make that statement is one of concurrence. But usually, the agreement assumes that magickal practitioners run around in witchy garb with big, long flowing robes and the women are all going to start wearing tons of gothic eye makeup.

From my viewpoint that's just fine if they want that. But most of the very accomplished magickal adepts I know dress pretty conservatively. Oh, they may get dressed up a bit eccentric at a gathering of other magickal adepts but generally the more accomplished adepts are, the more they are inclined to blend in day-to-day.

But a person's lifestyle can be changed by more than what clothing or cosmetics they wear. Frequently these changes take the form of increasing amounts of private time for reading and personal study. Many adepts I've known shy away from crowds. I'm not saying they become hermits.

Also, quite a number of them donate considerable amounts of time to activism for various causes as well as volunteer for community benefit events. These are just a few of the changes I have observed with dedicated and focused magickal adepts. There are many more some too subtle to mention here.

But one very common trait is this. With all the powers of the universe at their fingertips, none of the thirty or more serious magickal adepts I've known in my lifetime, use the magickal arts for their personal gain or to hurt someone.

But we'll talk about that in a chapter about ethics.

Part Two - Head Shaping

The Talking Self

Let's take a moment and discuss ourselves as the meat sock being, the proverbial TALKING SELF. The prose-poem below was written just as I was coming out of monastic life late 2004. It embodies the realizations of seven years of deep contemplation. I read it to one of my mystic teachers, and he smiled and said. "You get it!"

The Between Beast

We come from the great empty potential, plain and simple.

The force of our essence, a simple spirit instance of the divine, a pool of over souls, a simple individual soul, a soul body, yet with each layer of our spirit, we are simply a chip of the great empty potential.

It's only when we inhabit flesh, that we must take up the mechanics of the biology of that habitat realm. Only then are we loosely bound to the function of biology, only then are we loosely bound by culture, tradition, and the laws of man, only then must we be subject to sex and gender, and the tyranny of its control.

I've taken the challenge to question the nature of my flesh, I have taken the challenge to express who and what I am, I am a sexual fugitive and a gender outlaw!

I am not my flesh, I am not my biology, I am not a human having a spiritual experience, I am simply a spirit having a human experience. Know that I am simply an approximation of all that I am. For I am the shining light from within.

Know that I have taken many forms, many times; in many whens and many where's. My energy is made from emptiness, I am pregnant with universes, I am pregnant with all that is. I can radiate male, I can radiate female, I can radiate both, I can radiate all that is. My love is universal. For this is my nature.

Look past my flesh and see my true being. Look past the biology. For while I seem to be two spirits, know that I am much, much more. Know that I live between the genders, know that I live between the worlds, know that I live between the moments.

I am a Between Beast, hear me roar!

Please hear my soft, gentle words,

"This is simply my form, please love me as I am!"

(From a Prose-Poem originally written by Cheryl Costa 8/2004)

Analysis of the Poem

The body we inhabit, regardless of sex or gender or race is simply a costume we inhabit and wear, so that we can play in the game of physical reality.

The long and short of the poem is simply in the final analysis we are an eternal being, connected to everything, everywhere in every temporal aspect.

Since we are part of everyone, and everyone is part of us, the notion of being kind to one another is more than a mere courtesy. If we do hostile magic, we are simply hurting an aspect of ourselves. If we do benevolent magick we are simply being good to an aspect of ourselves. It's as simple as that.

In this context, our overarching theme should be:

Be kind, Be gentle, and Be Generous with your Magick.

Magickal Ethics

Definition of Ethics

1: ethics plural in form but singular or plural in construction: the discipline dealing with what is good and bad and with moral duty and obligation

2: a set of moral principles: a theory or system of moral values

Definition from: https://www.merriam-webster.com/dictionary/ethics

Here's where I'm coming from, my moral compass. I am a Priestess of the **Goddess ISIS**, I believe in Service, Sacrifice, Compassion and, Love unto all things.

My Wiccan brethren hold the following rede as a guide, ***"Do as you will harm none!"***

Over the years I've heard many other magickal practitioners, announce that they are NOT Wiccan that they do as they please with regards to magick.

When I published a small book of **Rules for New Magickal Students**, I received a volume of email that stated in essence, *"...we don't need no stinking rules..."*

A few years ago, I got a discussion going in a social media group about the Ethics of Magick. The tone of the discussion ranged from:

"We magickal adepts should live by a higher standard but *sometimes you have to break the rules!"*

"I use my own best judgement," or *"I'll do as I please,"*

and of course, the ever popular *"…we don't need no stinking rules…."*

But as a **Magickal Adept** I've always lived by the moral philosophy imparted to me as a child…and No, it didn't come from my Catholic school teachings. It came from ***Marvel Comics*** and the wisdom of the late Stan Lee.

"With great power comes great responsibility"

For magickal adepts this phrase has a simple meaning. *If you have the ability to do something, make sure that you do it for the good of others.*

I'll say this once, there is magickal blow back and there most certainly is a karmic impact for everything you do magickally.

My advice: BE KIND with your magick, BE GENTLE with your magick, BE GENEROUS with your magick.

Magick should be used for the benefit of your family, your neighbors, your community and the human family on this world. Notice I didn't say you. Magick works best when it is not self-serving.

Over the years I've had more than a dozen students who came to magick thinking that the magickal arts was a "big vending machine" where you could wish for anything you wanted and get it.

Still others approach the use of the magickal arts as a covert and personal weapon to trip up people they don't like, attack their personal enemies and perhaps destroy people they have made judgements about.

These days on various social media one cannot help but see almost daily posts of some magickal neophytes, asking for aggressive and most certainly attack spells. If one questions their justification, they almost always reply with a self-serving pronouncement. Usually, it's a statement that clearly indicates they have set themselves up as Judge, Jury and Vigilante Punisher. It's even more pervasive now with the *Cancel Culture.*

If you don't believe me, do a web search on how big the Black Magick industry is. It was a 3-Billion-dollar business, the last time I checked. That in itself says a lot about the ethics of people who utilize that industry's products.

Also, on social media it is common these days in some posting groups to see posts that claim that there is no such thing as magickal blow back. Frequently, the group administrators of these posting boards post policies that they don't believe in karma as well. Trust me when I say,

"Karma believes in you!" The Force knows if you've been naughty or nice!

Of course, people tell me that we should look to our world's religious deities and traditions for moral and ethical guidance. But after some research I think not. The Gods and Goddesses are just as messed up as are we. They're just a bit higher up the karmic ladder.

Another thing, and this comes directly from a Goddess I know and venerate.

"Stop asking us for stuff!

You have the same spark of life force we do.

Do it yourself!"

War and Peace

I was doing a little research for someone seeking a protection spell, but I found nothing related to a specific deity that you could call upon for the purpose of shielding you from physical harm by man, beast or magick. That said, some of the Bodhisattvas in the Buddhist tradition are considered Protectors. But most western Pagans generally wouldn't consider invoking Buddhist Bodhisattvas.

I decided to take the martial approach and looked at the War deities. Oh, there were plenty of them: brave, fierce, wrathful but none you could call upon to protect you. These deities were only war making oriented, and very suitable for attack magick.

Across 34 World Cultures, there were about 170 fierce war making Gods and Goddesses. I found this highly troubling. What does this say about our human species and the deities we as humans have venerated for eons?

Even the Christian God: Yahweh **Exodus 15:3**. (King James Version) ... *The Lord is a man of* ***war****: the Lord is his name.*

Add to that we get a good Idea of Yahweh's temperament in **Nahum 1:2** (Biblehub.com) *The LORD is a jealous and avenging God; the LORD is avenging and full of wrath. The LORD takes vengeance on His foes and reserves wrath for His enemies.*

In the back of my mind, I hoped and assumed that there had to be a balance between war making deities and the peace deities. It was a very bad assumption. Only 8 world cultures had Peace oriented deities. Represented by 11 Goddesses and 4 Gods. The cultural break-out of Peace deities went like this: 4-Greek, 1-Lakota, 1-Lithuanian, 1- Māori, 2-Norse, 1-Persian, 4-Roman and 1-Venezuelan

In the final analysis, I find myself returning to the moral ethic of Stan Lee, ***"With great power comes great responsibility."***

As I stated previously, for magickal adepts this phrase has a simple meaning; <u>if you have the ability to do something, make sure that you do it for the good of others.</u>

While I was in monastic life, I was taught a ritual process for ***"Raising the Great Abundance."*** The philosophy is simple but has wonderfully great implications. Many people practice magick only for themselves or their immediate family and friends. They literally are handing out the Magickal Benefit by the Spoonful.

Instead, consider raising that energy and offer it for the benefit of; <u>all beings, everywhere, everywhen</u>?

Think about this in a magickal ritual context. Raising power and offering purely for the benefit of all beings everywhere across the multiverse, in every temporal domain: past, present and future.

Every experienced Magickal Adept understands there is Magickal blow back: both positive and negative.

Do a questionable working and sooner or later it's going to bite you! Do a beneficial working and its blow back is going to be quite beneficial.

If you execute a beneficial ritual for zillions upon zillions of beings everywhere, wouldn't it make sense that the blow back would be abundant and positive for you? Can I hear a So Mote it be!

But I've lectured this topic for years and had some students rolling their eyes and saying, "I don't care about them other beings; I just worry about myself." So much for selfless magickal practice…and people wonder why I retired!

Cheryl's Ethical Rules

- **Do not practice attack Magick**
- **Be Kind**
- **Do unto others as you would do unto yourself**
- **Be Generous with your magick**
- **THINK BIG – THINK REALLY BIG with your magick**
- **Offer Great Magickal offerings for the benefit of all beings, everywhere, everywhen**
- **If you know protective magickal techniques, generously use them to protect the vulnerable.**

After thoughts: I hear some of you asking. *"Where do I find a book of Magickal Protective spells?"*

Let me say it this way, as Magickal Adepts we practice the art of turning **Thought into Form**.

Protective magick amounts to being creative. Visualize a magickal barrier of any sort around yourself or the person you are trying to protect. Again, it comes down to quieting one's mind and effectively visualizing. You need not light a single candle or burn a single stick of incense.

Personally, during meditation, I regularly wrap myself in magickal protective barriers and reinforce my previous protective wrappings.

My policy is I don't use attack magick. That said, I don't install attack aspects to my protective barriers either.

Magick is about heart, get your ego out of it

Over the years, I've known many new students who wanted to feel the exhilaration of working a piece of verifiable magick. Shortly after they do, they tend to get all cocky and present what I call the **"Great and Powerful Oz syndrome."** They develop an attitude like "I can do anything!"

Trust me, we've all been there, me included. Why does a beginner's initial magick work! But follow-on magickal efforts fall apart?

It's simple, really. Beginners start unsure of themselves. They usually approach magick with the innocence of a child, which is good. It's a humble, heartfelt drive to make it right and make it happen. As long as the magick is sincere and innocent, the magick works.

Once you start thinking you are all-powerful and your ego gets wrapped around the flagpole, losing your innocence along the way, the results of the conjuring effort go to pot, plain and simple.

That's why I use the baking of bread as a proxy tool in magickal training.

Bread making requires a relaxed manner. Bread making requires that you keep your focus and innocence during the effort. Start- getting sloppy, cut corners, and the bread will look like hell.

Magick and Bread making require focus, ethical practice, loving attention, and heart. Without heart there is no pride in your effort. An ego attitude – "I'm the best bread maker around, is not heart; the same goes for magick.

The heart requires a degree of innocence and humility. If your bread is first-class other people will talk up your product; the same goes for magick.

Heart is the key. Your heart and responsibility must be 100% into your magick or go home.

Let me be straightforward about this, not all pagans or witches are Magickal Adept material! I must be very clear about this. In fact, too many are just exploring or are in it for the party and the loose rules.

Many pagans, if you corner them about their theology, you'll get a grocery list of what they say they practice. Or they just tell you they're eclectic, a buzz word for, a little bit of this, and a little bit of that.

Most pagans that I have met will not claim the witch title. It's a position they presume will keep them pleasantly safe from dogmatic ridicule. In my experience most are not interested in becoming dedicated Magickal Adepts either.

Witches, Wiccans and a handful of other magickal traditions, on the other hand, tend to claim the title Witch or something of similar meaning, with all of its baggage. They make commitments, whether it's as a solitary practitioner or as a coven or circle member.

In essence, when a serious dedicated Adept makes their initiation bond with the Goddess, they are, in effect, taking vows.

Becoming a Magickal Adept doesn't require that you take vows, but it does require a strong constitution to accept failure, and a dedication to forge forward with your study and evolving practice.

Bottom line: Don't expect serious results in the magical arts if you aren't willing to make certain deep heartfelt commitments to the disciplines, the training regimen and the long-haul life practices of the magickal arts.

Fantastic Strangeness & Embracing the Quiet

With over 43 years of being in the CRAFT, I have found that most magickal students are always seeking the **"golden short cut"** in order for them to execute and manifest effective magick. This is evidenced by their huge collection of books on Magick Craft. They assume that somewhere, hidden in one of these magick books some other author is going to reveal an obscure sacred truth that will suddenly make Magick as easy as pie. **The truth is there is <u>no short cut.</u>**

A lot of people come to the Magickal Arts, thinking it's about lighting candles, burning incense, stuffing herbs and spells in little bottles, and dressing up in witchy robes. I find that sad. A significant number of students leave the class when they realize the learning of the Craft is a lot of commitment, study, head shaping, and just plain hard work.

What does this head shaping mean? It is about an elastic view of reality. Lots of people tell me they want to practice magick, but when you really talk to them, they frequently have a resistance to the idea that magick really does work. In the back of their minds, there is this deep-seated sense of resistance to the idea that they, as student practitioners can actually learn to bend reality.

So, this is where the head shaping aspect of magickal training starts. I call this series of lessons, an introduction to Fantastic Strangeness. It is a series of exercises to stretch your imagination. Hopefully, the result is that you will dare to imagine bigger things and appreciate stranger stuff. The intent is that you will overcome your disbelief, inhibitions, and fears; enough to dare to consider doing the impossible.

Western education did its best to literally beat inspired creativity out of us. Stripping us of our childhood boldness. Instilling in us a sense that we are insignificant. I frequently tell my students:

"Dare to think big! Dare to think really BIG!"

This sort of mind-stretching exercise typically starts perhaps with a moon circle or training circle. In the beginning, I ask those in attendance if they have any special intentions for the benefit from the magick that we raise.

It is typical as we go around the circle to hear each participant handing out the magickal benefit literally by the stingy spoonful. They want a little healing for some relative. Or they want a pinch of healing for their sick pet. Around the circle, each student meagerly assigning some tidbit of the magick for someone or for a particular intention. All of them not considering that we are talking about the limitless force of all creation. As the high priestess, I usually finish by saying, ***"I offer this magickal working for the benefit of all beings, everywhere, everywhen."***

The first time I do this with new students, you see looks of shock and awe on their faces. The exercise is intended to get the students to think of something bigger than themselves. To think of being of benefit to more living beings besides their immediate familiars.

Another way I try to stretch the reality of my students is to sit down and have "silly talk" with them. As a creative writer, I have to be able to think outside of the mundane reality box. I frequently ask students.

"Imagine if you will?" This or that situation or this strange and unusual place. Again, many initial students resist my efforts to be silly and in essence playful. If their resistance continues, they are usually encouraged to leave the class.

Rigidity tends to water down or even extinguish creative spontaneity. While magick requires certain disciplines, it also requires a healthy degree of creative spontaneity. Too much of each is not good, a balance is what is required. Buddha taught: Middle Path!

For the past twenty years, I have not begun student magickal training by starting with spellcasting! No! Absolutely Not!

I initially teach quietness practices that lead to evolving Divination skills and are focused on developing a personal connection and non-verbal dialog with the younger-self and by extension, the higher-self or cosmic consciousness.

Whether it is breadmaking, sitting meditation, walking meditation, playing with Legos™, playing with a tub of Play-Doh™ or listening to a bi-aural meditation inducement CD, our initial practical focus are quietness exercises.

You would be shocked how many students push back. They refuse to make a loaf of bread, meditate or play with toys or listen to a modern piece of meditation technology. *"This isn't real magick they tell me."*

They refuse to commit to a measly 2, 5, or 10 minutes of play or meditation daily and also keeping a daily journal of this activity. They whine, *"I don't have time, I'm too busy."*

From the resistance, you would think I was asking them to wear thumbscrews for some period each day. In my last couple of classes, I lost quite a few people who flat out told me, *"I think this play is childish" or "I find meditation just too darn hard!"*

Yes, I agree meditation is initially a lot of work. If it were easy, everyone would be doing it. Meditation quiets the chatter of our mundane minds. It gives us the ability to know the younger self. Meditation ends up being an exercise in improving the student's ability to do divining. Once you are grounded in meditation and developing divining as a way to communicate non-verbally with your younger self; your eventual practice of active spellcasting is much more efficient.

I have literally had students say to me during these divining and meditation exercises, *"When are we going to stop all this quietness, divining and ESP crap?"*

Resistance to learning these sorts of necessary mystical skills usually leads to a private consultation on why the student is in my class in the first place. The student is usually asked to suck it up and do as the rest of the class is doing or leave. Some leave.

My initial request of my students is for two minutes a day for two months of meditation. For some it's a hill too steep to climb, for some students is too small of an effort. They might state to me, *"Oh I can already do ten or twenty minutes of meditation."*

Or at least they think they can. There is a big difference between just sitting with your eyes closed and actually attempting to quiet your mind. This is what I call Drink from the fire hose syndrome. Frequently western students get this idea that "more is better." It is not!

If you attempt to jump into meditation for long periods at first, you will quickly find that you aren't actually doing it or give up stating that it's TOO HARD.

Why is it too HARD? Well, some students are afraid to be alone with their thoughts. Others won't confront and deal with the ghostly crap that comes up from their subconscious. Still others seem to think they can master it in a week. They cannot.

My rule: I'd rather have two good minutes of solid quiet meditation than 10 to 45 minutes of struggling. Approach meditation with the humbleness of a child.

All I am asking you to do is be quiet, and alone with your thoughts for a measly two minutes once a day, every day for at least a couple of months. Tiny Steps!

If the students actually engage the meditation practice, they begin telling me that: ***"all this crap keeps coming up!"***

Yep, it will, that crap is all the nonsense and worrying cycling and chattering around in your subconscious. Our two minutes a day is a tool to gradually quiet that chatter. This will give way to longer periods of quietness and eventually deep contemplation; Practice and Patience is the rule!

Elastic Reality Considerations for the Adept

In this essay, references to Witch, Wicca and Pagan, should be assumed to suggest the volume of people who are studying the Magickal arts to one degree or another. Likewise, some of what is discussed in this essay will challenge your world view. Keep in mind that a Magickal Adept has to be open to the high degree of strangeness in Reality.

In mid-2020 a major New York State newspaper published a feature article about the fact that in the past ten years, two dozen mainstream churches in their area have closed their doors. Related newspaper articles have pointed out that Folk Faiths like Wicca are the fastest growing religions in the country.

If we examine raw Facebook marketing numbers, on appearances they suggest that upwards of 4.6 million Wiccans are on Facebook. Yes, I hear you. Yes, I know you are probably in multiple Facebook Wiccan or Pagan groups. The Facebook Marketing people know that as well and naturally have highly massaged the Facebook Marketing data.

An advertiser seeking to purchase targeted promotion to a Wiccan audience is presented with two sets of numbers: Raw potential audience and tempered reasonable audience. So, for

Wiccans on Facebook, raw count 4.6 Million, tempered count about 1.7 million. Of course, not all USA Wiccans are on Facebook either, logic suggests that our numbers are somewhat bigger. Facebook Wiccans total about 1.7 million in the USA. The gender proportions work out to about 86% women and 14% men.

For the sake of simplicity let us use measured-tempered metrics to illustrate a point. The USA population is about 320 million, census data says 76% are adults, who would equate to about 243 million adults. Using the 1.7 million as a measured metric, and Facebook Wiccans roughly amount to about 2% of the USA adult population. That makes the Wiccan religion comparable in size with many smaller mainstream sects.

But if we consider the greater Pagan community as well, the numbers are more impressive. If we include Norse, Voodoo, Louisiana Voodoo, General Paganism, Wicca, Traditional Witchcraft, Druids, and Faery Traditions, the tempered Facebook total is about 48 million. That number in contrast to the 243 million US adults suggests that the overall pagan folk faith community totals about 20% in the USA.

What caused the Pagan Folk faiths to grow to be roughly one-fifth of the USA adult population?

The answer is a bit more complicated. There seems to be a montage of reasons but let us start with the Boomer generation. We Boomers were growing up in the 1950s. In the post-World War 2 world, rocketry was fascinating everybody. The press in those days regularly published news stories of UFO sighting accounts. The movies of the era were awash with space travel and the possibilities of aliens visiting our little blue planet. All of this forced the minds of both young and old to be a bit more elastic in our view of reality. Star Trek in the early 1960s and in the five decades since also contributed to this growth and a willingness to consider other possibilities.

What did this have to do with Craft and Pagan thought? It is about the impact on expanding of one's personal reality. A concept that challenged mainstream church and Sunday school teachings about reality.

In the 1960s women had no power in the outside world, especially in the religious world. The women's movement brought about the idea of inner power. Women began embracing a feminine face of deity. Of course, Pagan and Wiccan thought fed this view along with the ancient concepts of magick. The ability to bend reality with thought.

Likewise, in the 1960s, there was the tremendous influences of the musical group the Beatles. Their music changed a generation, with complex ideas and a degree of rebellion. Add to this, around 1967 the Beatles; John, Paul, George, and Ringo, became fascinated with the Transcendental Meditation teachings of Indian Yogi guru, Maharishi Mahesh. In 1968, they visited the Maharishi's spiritual training camp in Rishikesh, India.

The immense popularity of everything Beatles, brought Transcendental Meditation to the west. At the time, mainstream western clergy were absolutely appalled by this far eastern influence. But the Beatles made these eastern concepts "Hip!" Again, another stimulus to the idea of mind-altering thought and reality expansion.

Before we leave the 1960s, we must also consider the impact that hallucinogenic substances of that era had on the young adult boomer population. A late government physicist friend of mine once observed that the government was against recreational drug use because it helps you experience an alternate reality, which makes you start to question things, including the government.

Since the 1960's the better part of two additional generations have been influenced by an ever-expanding paradigm shift. A shift that made our collective realities more elastic.

We are all magickal people here. Let's take a walk on the wild side. I hesitate to share the following, but I think it has bearing on something bigger that has been afoot for a long time.

> "For many individuals who have seen a UAP/UFO, have had a near-death experience (NDE), or an out of body experience (OBE), or even have had direct physical contact with non-human intelligence (NHI), your life is never the same after this event." (Mitchell Foundation, 2018. **Beyond UFOs – The Science of Consciousness in Contact with Non—Human Intelligence -** Published by FREE.)

This is a profound statement! It suggests that the mere experience of seeing a UAP/UFO can trigger deep psycho-spiritual changes in the witness. As a journalist I have read many hundreds of UFO sighting reports. Often the reporting individuals stated they had never taken the subject of UFOs seriously before. Then they experienced an extraordinary sighting event. These same people frequently report that it profoundly changed them.

> Of 3256 experiencers/abductees surveyed by the Dr. Mitchell Foundation, most reported that their experiencer event greatly altered their view of reality, of religion and most certainly, of spirituality.
>
> Reinerio Hernandez, co-founder of FREE, told me that he knew dyed in the wool scripture thumpers who came back from their ET experience deeply spiritual. Likewise, atheists and agnostics who were touched by ET and returned intensely spiritual. Then Mr. Hernandez remarked, *"ET seems intent on turning everybody into mystics!"*

To quote a variant of a Wiccan chant, *"ET is trying to touch everybody and everybody that ET touches Changes."*

Mystics! That struck a chord with me. I spent seven years of my mid-life in a Buddhist monastery. During my mystical training, a seasoned Lama told me. *"Most people have no idea the high degree of paranormal phenomena that goes on around them every day. Most people only need to stretch the boundaries of their reality a little bit to be aware of a much bigger world."*

So how many people has ET touched by simply appearing in the sky for our mortal eyes to see?

That is a tough question. But being a statistician, I took a crack at the numbers. In the last, twenty years there's been roughly 167,632 reported UAP/UFO sightings. The sightings were reported principally to two national reporting services. But honestly, 167K reports doesn't exactly put a dent into the human population if ET is trying to launch humankind on the road to mystical enlightenment.

But in July of 2017, FOX Home Entertainment conducted a national poll about UAP/UFOs and ET. The results were like a 2012 poll by National Geographic that said 36% of Americans believe in UAP/UFOS, 42% were on the fence about the topic, and 17% thought the topic was nonsense.

But the FOX Home Entertainment poll went a step further and asked how many had seen a UAP/UFO. The result was measured at about 16% of adult Americans. This 16% number was a measurable metric. Then in September 2019, a Gallup Poll did yet another poll on the UAP/UFO topic and they too measured the number of people who said they had seen a UAP/UFO, again the 16% number was now a stable measured metric.

The US population is about 328 million people. The adult population is approximately 76% of the total, or about 250 million people. Sixteen percent of the adult population works out to roughly about 40 million people. That is a lot of people potentially on the road to being ET initiated mystics. That's 40 million people who have had their view of reality expanded just by having an unexplainable UFO sighting experience. This doesn't begin to address the number of people who have been actual physical guests of ET, namely the abductees and experiencers.

When I first wrote a UFO related newspaper blog-column in 2013, I was under the common impression that ET physical contact was a very rare thing. Then I had the opportunity to attend a daily experiencers meeting at a UFO conference. To be honest, I expected to meet 25 or 30 people crying in their coffee that they got probed by ET. To my surprise, there were about 150-175 people at the meeting. It had all the high energy of a tent revival! The average experiencer told me, *"Those ET folks are great! They want the best for us and want us to save our planet!"*

So why is ET routinely flying over our hamlets, villages, towns, and mega cities? If this mystical agenda is at the heart of it, then maybe ET are gently trying to coax our human species to be a little bit more elastic in our view. Perhaps their hope is that we'll all gradually wake up to a much bigger reality and join the other citizens of the universe.

Afterthoughts

I want all of you reading this to remember I'm presenting Advanced Mystical concepts. Please understand that the deeper you go into Meditation, Mystical Contemplation and the general study of Advanced Magick; the weirder it will get.

An advanced student and I hit head-to-head brutally after I exposed a recent yearlong Magickal Class to this essay. At issue was that I exposed the class to a little bit of UFO theory. That advanced student refused to confront or even entertain that there might be other life in the universe and that perhaps it's visited us on our little blue planet. That screamed rigidity! Rigidity poisons thinking in Advanced Mystical Studies.

UFO theory was inserted to stretch your reality a bit. My job as an instructor is to stretch you. Remember, I told you all, that working in mysticism requires you to have an elastic view of reality. Put the following quote in your magickal journals or Grimoires.

"Not only is the universe stranger than we think, but it is also stranger than we can think."

— Werner Heisenberg – German theoretical physicist and one of the key pioneers of quantum mechanics.

Part Three-The Mechanics of Magick

Meditation and the Maharishi Effect

Most of us, when we started our magickal training, learned that reality is flexible and malleable. Meaning that we can bend reality with the power of our thoughts. The whole practice of magick is about the art of bending reality to our will with our thoughts.

A lot of people have this view of the craft that it's all spellcasting, candles, chanting, and crystals. I've observed over the years that anyone seriously involved with witchcraft learns that a smart witch learns the art of quieting oneself.

Many of our rituals are, in effect, processes that numb the ordinary conscious mind. They allow for deeper, thoughtful, and a creative mind to take charge and do the actual magickal work.

In high school physics class, they taught us that neither **energy** nor **matter** can be destroyed. This means that matter can change into energy, and vice versa, energy can be converted into matter. That's the mundane scientific explanation.

In the Buddhist view, we deal with the terms: **form** and **emptiness**. Emptiness is the energy/potential and the **great potential** to be anything that thought can manifest. **Form** is the manifestation of that thought that is powered by the limitless potential of emptiness. From one of the common Buddhist Sutras, it says: *"Form is emptiness and emptiness is none other than form."*

The view is that form arises from emptiness given the direction of thought. We as magical people understand that our words and our thoughts can take form. Many of my early teachers cautioned my peers and me: once you start practicing a magical lifestyle, be careful what you think and be careful what you say. In simpler terms, be careful what you ask for; you very likely may get it.

As I mentioned earlier, much of what we do in spellcasting and in our rituals are mechanisms to quiet our day to day chattering mind. This allows us to touch a deeper transcendent aspect of our greater mind and consciousness.

If we were on a small rowboat out on the ocean and suddenly, the waves began to rise around us 10, 20 maybe 50 feet in height, we might become alarmed that the ocean is raging all around us. But when you consider that the ocean is many miles deep, if you were to take a cross-section of these many miles in-depth piece of ocean, you would notice that the waves on the surface are only a minuscule part of the overall ocean. For the most part, the ocean is more or less quiet and settled.

If we look at our own mind, we find that it's very much like the ocean. All of our day to day, busy things and rushing around in circles is represented by the waves on top of the ocean. From the perspective of our little rowboat, the waves are big, wild, and violent.

But what most people don't understand is that, overall, our state of mind is as deep as the ocean. Once we get below the daily churn of the thinking mind, we find quieter states.

If we practice any number of meditative techniques, we can quiet our minds and discover those deep depths of consciousness. It's in these deepest depths that aspects of our greater mind hold our dreams, our creativity, unlimited intelligence, boundless happiness, focus, and most certainly clarity. I had a Buddhist lama once tell me that within the deepest depths of our quiet mind is the unlimited potential to manifest anything.

If we teach ourselves to meditate and work ourselves up to a daily practice of about 20 minutes per day, amazing things happen to our minds, the nature of our thinking, and the collateral benefit to our mind-body connection.

These days many mental health experts tell us the more we quiet our minds, the more profoundly the effect shows up as a physical response in our bodies. Meditation can give us this deeper level of mental rest—much more than the deepest sleep. There have been more than over 300 academic and research peer-reviewed studies on Meditation and its remarkable impacts on our mental health and our overall body health.

In 2014, the Department of Defense-sponsored a 2.4-million-dollar study to explore Transcendental Meditation as a tool for Warrior Wellness in combating Post Traumatic Stress Syndrome or PTSD.

During my seven years of Buddhist monastic life, I learned deep meditation practices. These practices made it possible for me to tame the lingering aspects of my combat service PTSD. As a result, I finally found peace.

As well, the practice of Meditation has significantly impacted and improved the quality of my divining and ongoing magickal work. If you want to be a serious-minded magickal practitioner, some form of Meditation is the key.

The shame of it is that many of my students tell me, *"Oh, I do not have time to meditate, I'm too busy."* What they fail to grasp is the benefit to their own wellbeing. Meditation helps to tame the monkey chatter in our minds. This chatter contributes to stress that causes many of the everyday ailments that people complain about. Why? Because our thoughts are so keyed up with to-do-lists that we rarely get a chance to settle down.

But for the witch who lives by the credo that **"Witches Heal."** Here is another excellent reason a witch should learn to meditate.

The Maharishi Effect

Earlier, I wrote about expanding your perception of reality and making your view much more elastic. In that essay, I spoke of the musical group the Beatles.

Back in 1968, John, Paul, George, and Ringo of the Beatles became influenced by the Transcendental Meditation teachings of Indian Teacher Maharishi Mahesh yogi. They even spent a considerable amount of time at Maharishi's compound in Rishikesh in northern India to take part in a Transcendental Meditation™ training course.

So just what is the Maharishi Effect?

Yogi Maharishi Mahesh predicted back in 1960 that if 1% of a population were practicing Transcendental Meditation™ techniques, there would be a measurable improvement in the quality of life for the whole community.

In a 1976 published research paper, it was reported that in 1974 this Maharishi effect was detected and measured. The observation was that when 1% of the community practiced transcendental meditation techniques, there was a measurable drop in the local crime rate. The research paper noted a reduction in the local crime rate, which was measured at an average of 16% lower. This same research paper coined the term the Maharishi Effect.

If we struggle for a definition, the Maharishi Effect can be said to be an influence of coherence and projection of positivity into the local societal and regional environment. Manifested by a large group of persons practicing Meditation in general and/or specifically a group of TM-Sidhi™ program practitioners practicing regionally at a time.

This is very intriguing. For over thirty years, I have had the motto: **Witchcraft is an Art, a Science, and a Lifestyle.** Here is yet another illustration of mystical-meets-science from the Maharishi Effect research.

"On the basis of analogies to physical systems, scientists estimated that the coherence generated by group practice of the TM-Sidhi program should be proportional to the square of the number of participants. Considering the "1%" finding, it was predicted that a group with size equal to the square root of 1% of a population would have a measurable influence on the quality of life of that population. For example, a group of 200 practicing the TM-Sidhi program together in a city of four million (100 x 200 x 200) would be sufficient to produce a measurable influence on the whole city; a group of 1,600 in the U.S. would influence 256 million (100 x 1600 x 1600) people, the whole population of the U.S.; and a group of 7,000 would influence 4.9 billion (100 x 7000 x 7000) people, the population of the world at that time."
(https://research.miu.edu/maharishi-effect/ Retrieved 6/10/2020)

Let us put this in Witch Terms. Imagine a group of say <u>five witches</u> all well trained in a specific style of Meditation similar to TM-Sidhi. Using the ratios previously stated (100x5x5) could have an impact on a small-town of 2500 people.

Let us take this a step further. Imagine a group coven of perhaps <u>thirteen witches,</u> all well trained in a specific style of Meditation similar to TM-Sidhi. Using the ratios previously stated (100x13x13) could have an impact on a small-town of 16,900 people (17K).

Now if we gently dare to think BIG. Imagine a Wiccan clan of 10 hive covens with 10 members each or <u>100 witches,</u> all well trained in a specific style of Meditation similar to TM-Sidhi. Using the ratios previously stated (100x100x100) could have an impact on a city or county of 1 million people. Imagine the societal benefits.

If we, as Magickal practitioners, expand our view of how we can advance the practice of our mystical art, imagine the things we could change for the better.

Connectivity - Magickal Direction & Targeting

In a previous essay about Magickal Mechanics, I stated that: "Our life spark is connected to the great consciousness and therefore everything, everywhere, everywhen. We are not separate from it."

The question has been raised to me. "If we're so connected to everything, why can't I touch an Alien on Zeta Reticuli, 39 light years away?" Well in pure theory you can. It's not impossible but it does require a quieter mind. As well there are other factors that must be considered that inhibit that sort of deeper connection.

Ok let's take this in Baby Steps. Let us talk about this topic with the metaphor of schools of fish in the Ocean. Think of the Great Consciousness as similar to the collective Oceans on the Earth. Within our ocean system there are zillions of fish swimming in big and small schools.

It is often said in mysticism that we are connected to an immediate local group of spirit instances. Lifetime after lifetime we reincarnate together. My daughter in this lifetime may have been my mother in a previous life or perhaps my military Captain, or simply a colleague in a common profession, perhaps even a vicious enemy, who knows. Lifetime after lifetime we all wear different masks-of-flesh and participate in this Game of Incarnate life.

This cluster of these spirits can be metaphorically considered like a local school of fish. Things that happen to any of us affects the others. If a member of the school moves one way, many times the whole school will follow suit. Likewise, most the time the school just seems to function almost as one common entity. By extension all the schools of spirit entities throughout the ocean-of-consciousness pretty much function as collective spiritual societies unto themselves.

In practical magickal terms many of us have had requests to do healing workings for some person's sick relative. Many times, this request comes via multiple degrees of separation. In the end we, the practitioners usually have virtually no direct channel of connection to the critically sick person.

Classically, we Magickal Adepts have asked for something that is intimately connected to the person in question. Therefore, we Adepts might ask for something they may have worn recently, maybe a lock of their hair, or their fingernail clippings. I used to know an Adept who used to ask for a drop of the sick person's blood. Of course, these days with infections like Covid-19 and its many variants, gathering personal items, locks of hair or nail clippings, or infected body fluids is very risky.

Many years ago, in monastery life, we monastics frequently received requests for Karma changing magick all the time, in the form of Fire Pujas, a grand fire offering ritual. One of our requirements was a "blood connection." How was this done? At a very minimum a "blood relative" would purchase a large quantity of grain offerings that would be offered in the great fire pit during the ritual proceedings.

The more acute the situation, the greater the need for deeper blood connection with additional blood relatives present. If the situation was "gravely" serious, the requirement would be for multiple blood relatives to be in attendance and actively participating in the ritual proceedings.

As Adepts we rarely have an adept blood relative of a gravely sick individual wanting to participate with a large circle working on their behalf. In that regard I use <u>the young and innocent model</u>.

Since I have no direct connection to the sick relative, I usually write a prayer specifically for that sick person's situation and request that the family have a child of 6-8 years of age, who dearly loves that sick person make the prayer offering.

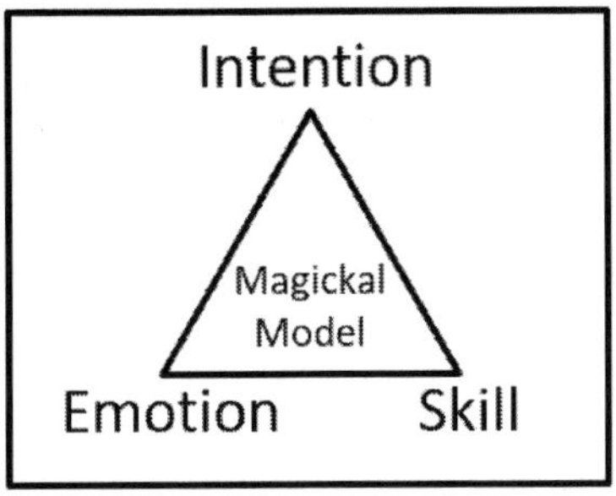

My magickal thinking calls upon the simplest of magical models. First, we always must have clear **Intention.** Then we must have a strong **emotional** connection to the Intended Recipient. If we do not have a clear path of relationship or an emotional connection, we as Adepts must rely on a combination of **magickal skills and techniques**.

In my experience, I would rather have the emotional energy of a teary eyed seven-year-old little girl who dearly loves her grandmother saying the healing prayer, over my circle of disinterested Adept strangers. Likewise, I would rather have a half dozen old ladies from the grandmother's parish who know her and are willing to come and do a group rosary for her. This is a friendly group connection and an intense mantra like recitation ritual. Both are powerful stuff.

Again, <u>Connection is Everything</u>. But let us examine another approach to establishing connection.

We have already talked about classic **Contagious magick** using things a person once had contact with items of clothing, locks of hair, fingernail clippings, a drop of blood, perhaps teeth, perhaps that person's fingerprint.

Of course, there is the concept of **Sympathetic magick,** a magick principle based on correspondence and/or imitation.

Let us look at Sympathetic magic on the principle of **imitation**. Most of us have seen the movie portrayal of someone using the classic poppet or VooDoo doll. Typically, we see the action of sticking pins into the Voodoo doll that acts as a proxy for the actual person. The effects of sticking in a pin into the proxy directly affects the target. Of course, this imitation approach requires serious focus on the part of the adept practitioner. This is an example of Sympathetic magick's nature of "Like produces Like."

Another approach using **Sympathetic magick** is the principle of **correspondence.** During my early training, some forty years ago, teachers rarely explained the concept of correspondence beyond being a form of imitation using a vegetable as the poppet instead of making a doll.

But there is a more modern approach to look at the principle of correspondence. That is from the perspective of divining.

I can take a photograph of a statue of George Washington in the city square, stuff it into an envelope, seal it, then put a random number or random alpha-numeric on the outside of the envelope. We now have a correspondence link between that number and that statue of George Washington in the city square.

If we give that random number to a group of Diviners or Remote viewers, it's possible to discern very accurate information about the target in the envelope without having seen it.

If I were to write down on a 3x5 card the precise latitude and longitude of the Eiffel Tower and stuff that into an envelope, seal it and assign a random number to it, the Diviner and Remote viewers again might start describing the iron work and people milling around the structure and perhaps even start doodling imagery that resembles the Eiffel Tower.

The US ARMY and the CIA discovered this phenomenon back in the early 1970s. Publicly nobody knows how this association principle works, but it just does! As Magickal Adepts we clearly understand that everything is connected. The mere name of the target is a minimal connection channel.

Finally, if I were to write on a 3x5 card: "Visit Tranquility Base on the Moon on July 20, 1969," stuff that into an envelope, seal it and assign a random number to it, the Diviners and Remote viewers again might start describing a bright, desolate place, far away, and perhaps remark it looks like clowns in puffy suits hopping around with a flag. YES, really! Those are the words of one of my students many years ago.

Is it not interesting? With no obvious connection, using only a Target number, we took our Diviners and Remote viewers across both Time and Space. This is an example of how we immortal spirits living in our human bodies on this little Blue planet can reach out and touch things across the cosmos.

The remarkable thing about using the Target Number technique, is that it works both ways. It works as a tool for divining and for active magickal workings. Think of it, both Solitary and Group magickal practitioners can focus magickal energy toward a target inside that envelope with wonderful effect. There are some procedural rules of the road and ethical considerations that must be followed but the correspondence principle works very effectively in this regard.

Let's go back and examine a previous problem. Earlier our group circle had no good connection to a sick person. Imagine taking a photo of the sick grandma who is in her ICU bed, stuff that photo into an envelope, seal it and assign a random number to it. Then have a circle of Adepts over to direct healing energy directly to that specific target number. If the situation is serious enough, you could post the random number sequence on social media so that many others can direct magickal energy to the target. Since her identity is anonymously sealed in an envelope, no one but the managing

Magickal Adept needs to even know who the healing is for, thus protecting the woman's HIPAA privacy.

Technical Kinks Related to Extreme Distance Viewing/Magickal Targeting

In my previous essay about Connectivity, I said, our life spark is connected to the great consciousness and therefore everything, everywhere, everywhen. In theory we should be able to shift our consciousness to any point of Time and Space. In theory, yes. But in applied practice there are some nagging kinks.

For about twenty years I taught classes in Remote Viewing or RV to my students and others from the pagan community. Now I hear some Adept-oriented people moaning "Remote Viewing is not Adept craft, it's not the old ways." I beg to differ. Think of it as a modern disciplined procedure-based approach to old school divining.

If you search on the internet, you might find some excellent web sites on RV. Also, you will find some New Age sites that proclaim that remote viewing is some sort of grand psychic gift that yields great colorful visions and communing with the spirits etc. Nothing could be further from the truth!

First off real remote viewing ***"Has all the charm of trying to see a cow through a bucket of mud"*** as one esteemed RV instructor put it.

Real remote viewing has been described as the ability to data mine accurate information about a non-local place, person, or an event without using one's physical senses or any other obvious means. There are NO big colorful visions!

The basic principle behind the technique states that we as living beings all have an immortal spirit that is connected to everything. By use of a Blind Target cue, a Remote Viewer is targeted to a specific place, or time or to a specific item.

How this works. I as a proctor-instructor arrange in advance for target items to be stuffed into envelopes. Several times over the years my wife has had one of her interns make target cues for me. One intern would cut pictures out of the newspaper, write target cards, even take pictures on their phones of items at home or in the office, and make hard copies. Then hand those target items off to another intern who would dutifully stuff and seal the individual cards in blank envelopes.

Finally, a third intern would sit down with a computer and a random number generator and assign target cue random numbers on each blank envelope. This is called triple blind. Even I the Proctor, have no idea what Targets are in what envelopes. Typically, the interns generate a stack of perhaps 100 target envelopes. This is done to provide a high degree of randomness.

All of these envelopes are put into a sack or a tub for a random drawing at class time or at a team practice time. Later at a classroom session or an Away-Team RV session, we meditate everyone into a calm state of quietness or the "Zone." Then, I as proctor remove a random target card, state the target number three times, and begin to walk the participants through the very structured set of Remote Viewing protocols or Stages that are designed to progressively mine more and more information about the selected target in layers of information.

For the record. Over twenty years, I have had 5 or 6 self-proclaimed seers or psychics visit a session and fail miserably in their attempt to gather information about the Targets. On the other hand, the RV class students or the Away-team, would generate pages, and pages of verifiable information.

What is an Away-Team? The idea was garnered from Star Trek™. During classes we figured out that some RV viewers seem to "click" with the environment of the target, others pick up on the energetics of the site. Still others are adept at describing and drawing the target.

Lastly some RV viewers tend to lock on to living beings. I know at least two viewers who routinely end up in the cockpit of the jet plane, or the space suit of the astronaut, or perhaps mingle with the customers at a French café in Paris in the 1920s. Later during post viewing analysis, the combined data results illustrate a comprehensive assessment of the target.

What does any of this have to do with Adept craft? Put simply, "The Limits-Phenomenon."

In the beginning of this essay, I stated that we are connected to everything, everywhere, everywhen. In theory any of the Remote Viewers should be able to go to any target that is presented. Yet, over the years I noted some viewers could not go to certain places. Remember the targets are blind to all of us until we open the sealed envelope during after session analysis.

The scenario would go like this. We start our normal process and somewhere during the first stage a viewer puts down their pen. Typically, I would ask the viewer to try probing the target Glyph generated by the Younger self again. Normally a viewer would pick up their pen and try again. If they still put the pen down, I used to suspect they could not touch the target. Later during the analysis when the Target card was removed and revealed, the target was usually some arduous location. For example: Visiting the RMS Titanic where it is now. It is important to note that the remains of the great ship are under 12,600 feet of water.

Over time I noted that when attempting to reach a more hazardous target environment, one or more viewers would put their pens down and stop the viewing efforts. These difficult targets were rare, but the behavior was consistent. Over a period of ten years, after many classes and away-team sessions the pattern became strong. Some very good viewers just could not visit certain targets.

In the end it seemed to come down to two things: a reservation to explore targets of extraordinary distance, and the fear of ordinary life-threatening environments. In both cases this equated to a Natural Self-Preservation response.

In terms of Self Preservation, if the Target was a highly hazardous or deadly environment some people reacted with a fear-based response. It is important to remember that the viewers do not consciously know what the target is. Logic would suggest that at a subconscious level they clearly know, and their natural self-preservation responses kick in.

If the Target was visiting the Chernobyl melt down, Tranquility base on the moon or visiting Opportunity on Mars, many of the viewers put their pens down. One viewer regarding the Chernobyl target scribbled in his margin notes, "I'll die." Another viewer on his Tranquility base target wrote in his session notes: "There's no air."

Finally, in one of my classes 5 of 6 viewers put their pens down. One person didn't throw their pen down on the table. The Target was "Opportunity on Mars." Three viewer students made margin notes that suggested that the target was "Too Far" or "I can't go that far away…"

Over time, many viewers, if they had kept up with RV class exercises, seemed to train their subconscious that visiting such dangerous targets was not a threat to their physical presence. Likewise traveling very great distances was not problematic either. Or was it?

In 2013, I invited some of my best remote viewers to a Sunday afternoon "Difficult Targets Away Team Party." There were seven viewers. I had a collection of color-coded target cards, that I knew all had great distances associated with them. I did not know what the targets were, only that they involved excessive distances. They did not come out in any particular order.

The International Space station was a piece of cake. An old Apollo moon landing site, no problem. A trip to Mars to find the rover "Spirit." One person could not accomplish it.

The target of "The Water Geysers" on Saturn's moon, Enceladus. Half the team put down their pens. One person scribbled, "I can't it's too far."

The last target was the Voyager 1 space craft. At that time, the space craft was 7,143,016,613 miles from Earth. Radio signals sent from the craft took a little over ten hours to get here. Six of the seven viewers put down their pens, they could not touch Voyager 1. Two viewers wrote in their notes, "too far" or "I'll lose my way back."

One viewer touched it. As a matter of fact, she crawled all over it, sketching details and writing descriptions. She clearly had acquired the target. What was different about her?

One, she regularly meditated and knew how to deeply quiet herself. Two, she was also the <u>only Adept</u> in the group and a well-seasoned Adept at that.

Could any Adept have done it? Probably not, because not all Adepts are rambunctious risk takers. Many experienced Adepts are, but certainly not all. This exceptional lady is clearly a risk taker and was willing to reach out and go for broke!

In the beginning of this chapter, I asked the question: "If we're so <u>connected</u> to everything, why can't I touch an Alien on Zeta Reticuli, 39 light years away?" **Answer:** Fear, Self-Preservation and a fear of taking risks.

So, after much consideration…

Again, can we touch an Alien on Zeta Reticuli, 39 light years away? Perhaps we can with the following:

- Good Deep Meditation skills,
- Serious Remote Viewing Training,
- Sub-conscious Fears Dampening,
- and above all Commitment and Patience.

Intro to Meditation Techniques

People are always asking me: What's the best type of meditative technique?

To be honest with you, they all accomplish the task of quieting the mind. The thing to keep in mind is that meditation is the habitual process of training your mind. The meditation process is intended to focus and redirect your thoughts.

So why do we as Magickal Adepts want to meditate?

Keep in mind that we live in a complex, busy, and at times chaotic western culture. First off consider the chore of driving on a busy expressway, it can be rattling especially with cars dodging in and out of lanes; it's insane.

Add to that, these days you can't walk into some restaurants without four or five television screen feeds with sports events or news channels visually attracting our attention.

Consider how many times a day you bow your head and focus attention on some social media feed on your phone.

Consider the stresses of whatever form of employment you are engaged in.

Finally, family, friends and social life pulls us in a dozen directions, places and adds more demands on our time and our mind space. All of the aforementioned life distractions are an impediment to the type of metaphysical skills we want to have and the wonderful work we wish to do.

The biggest challenge to us Magickal Adepts is that we must acquire the skill to focus our mind and quiet ourselves in order to perform magickal practices.

Balance is the Key! Balancing Mystical life with personal and family life, duties and responsibilities.

Some Health Benefits to Meditation

As I stated in another chapter modern science has documented that regular Meditation has significant health benefits.

For example: regular meditation practice will reduce your overall stress levels. High stress levels can affect your sleep patterns, increase anxiety level and most certainly promote depression. Stress can and does increase blood pressure levels and fatigue.

Regular habitual exercise of mindfulness and meditation practices has a significant impact on reducing all of the health issues I just mentioned.

Other benefits of daily meditation practices include increased attention spans and focus, as well as an improved self-image and self-worth feeling.

The only challenge is that **YOU HAVE TO DO IT!** Not once in a while but daily.

Let's take a moment and talk about carving out time to meditate.

In a previous essay I suggested that two minutes at first was a good start. The notion of methodically doing two minutes of quieting per day sounds easy. It's not! The reason I pitch the two minutes of quietness every day for two months is to establish and entrench the habit.

Since I mentioned health benefits related to meditation, think of the daily two minutes or more as an exercise of PAYING yourself first with a few minutes of quiet and peace.

During several yearlong classes, I checked in with my students and asked them on social media, "What's your meditation status." During the first few months, they report shaky but improving practice. Then I stopped asking. I came back 3-4 months later and asked. The answers were essentially, a bunch of sheepish "I forgot." Again, the demands of our busy-busy western culture took priority, and the meditation session was deferred to "later," <u>but later never came</u>.

Only one student claimed solid daily practice, which she backed up with journal entries and notes.

I can't force you to do daily meditation practices. But becoming a serious and accomplished Magickal Adept has to be your objective and the driving reason to do it, period. As I've told my students in the past: establishing a firm but flexible discipline with regards to your daily meditation practice is one of those MUST DO THINGS, if you are going to be a first-class Magickal Adept.

"You won't become a Jedi Knight if you don't practice meditation and quietness daily, nor will you become a Jedi Knight by fussing with your phone a hundred times a day."

Enough said!

Types of Meditation

I'm not actually going to do much more than a basic meditation instruction. There are plenty of good books on the basic types. I'll leave that to your own research and study.

Meditative Techniques have been around since ancient times. If you do a web search you will be swamped with lists of different types of meditation. Ranging from 3 types to up to 28 types of meditation techniques. For example: 1. Mindfulness meditation, 2. Spiritual meditation, 3. Focused meditation, 4. Movement meditation, 5. Mantra meditation, 6. Transcendental Meditation, 7. Progressive relaxation, 8. Loving-kindness meditation.

To be honest with you most of what you'll see are all *marketing spins.*

Most serious books on Meditation will expose you to the three basic types I learned in monastery. They are Sitting Meditation, Standing Meditation, and Walking Meditation.

Sitting Meditation

Sitting Meditation is just that. Most commonly when people think of meditation, they have a mental picture of someone sitting in a rigid lotus position. I've done plenty of time in lotus positions. Lotus positions are great if you are young and limber. In my mid-forties, I found that the lotus position was affecting the circulation in my legs. Why? I am a diabetic. Diabetics have higher glucose levels and therefore their blood tends to be thicker and that affects blood circulation. Also, folks with arthritic issues will find a classic lotus painful and troublesome. I find that I can meditate just fine sitting on a small stool or in a typical straight back dining room chair. My advice is to avoid meditating in overstuffed furniture like easy chairs or couches. There is a tendency to get too comfortable and fall asleep. While sitting, you do simple breath exercises to give yourself a quieting rhythm. The other thing you can do is perform mantra recitations while thumbing through some mala beads in your hand.

Standing Meditation

Standing meditation is just that. You do everything you would do in

Sitting Meditation, but you do it standing up. When I worked 2nd shift, I used to come home from work, park the car in the garage and close the door. Then I would stand in the driveway and do 5-10 minutes of Standing Meditation to relax out the stress issues of a night's problems at work or dealing with traffic chaos driving home. These days when the weather is nice, I walk out on to my apartment's balcony, close the door behind me and just stand there for 10-20 minutes doing my meditative breathing exercises. Typically, after I have put a roast or a bird or bread in the oven, I've got 45-90 minutes to kill while the meat cooks and bread bakes. This is the art of managing your idle time.

Walking Meditation

Walking Meditation is especially nice in a peaceful park or arboretum. My wife and I frequently do Walking Meditations in our neighborhood. At this writing, we live in upstate New York and during nice weather do our Walking Meditations along the old Erie Canal. Many people, including me, perform mantra recitations while thumbing through some mala beads in my hand.

During my monastic days, I lived for a time with a group of Burmese Monks and Nuns. Our walking meditations frequently were simple mantra recitations while thumbing through our individual mala beads. Sometimes the senior monk would lead us in softly singing the repetitious mantra as we walked through a local park.

These are all classic forms of meditation posture, none of them had any other intent but to practice mindfulness and mental quietness. Ok, I hear some of you saying: singing for quietness? Actually yes. The mantra repetition and the walking pace were similar to breathing exercises. The repetition of the mantra is quite mentally numbing, in essence, quieting. In Catholic terms think of it like saying a group rosary. It's similar meditative mechanics.

Modern Techniques

The aforementioned meditation techniques are classic and have stood the test of time. But we as modern Magickal Adepts should take advantage of new modern techniques as well.

The technology is called Binaural Beats. In 1839, Heinrich Wilhelm Dove a Prussian physicist and meteorologist discovered Binaural tones. Very little was done with this discovery until 1973 when Robert Monroe and his development team rediscovered the incredible potential of binaural tones to influence human consciousness.

Monroe's team discovered that, depending on what consciousness state you want to achieve, you have to listen to a specific combination of binaural frequencies. He and his team experimented around with binaural beats and in 1975 created the Hemi-Sync™ technology. In his first laboratory and later in the Robert Monroe Institute he and his team created exercise after exercise and tested his Hemi-Sync combinations on thousands of people.

Binaural Beats work like this: Using stereo headphones, you play one tone of, perhaps, 108 Hz into one ear and a similar tone of 100 Hz into the other ear.

If you were to hear the tones separately you would hear a steady tone. But when you hear the two tones simultaneously coming from opposite directions you start perceiving a vibrato or wavering sound. This is when your brain becomes synchronized – your brain hemispheres work in unison. The wavering tone is the signal or proof that the brain is creating a binaural beat, in our example at exactly 8 Hz – the difference between the two tones.

Our brains cannot be influenced with sound waves directly because we cannot hear the frequencies which could influence our brain.

Our Brain Frequencies

The frequencies of our brains vibrate somewhere between 1 and 30 Hz depending on our state of consciousness. Right now, as you read this, your brain waves vibrate somewhere between 14 and 30 Hz, known as the Beta brainwaves.

In a relaxed, state our Alpha brainwaves range between 7 to 14 Hz. Of course, in humans, our audio hearing range starts at 20 Hz and ends at about 20,000 Hz so we can't hear the binaural tones.

In order to influence our brain with sound for relaxation, meditation, creativity, sleep, and so on, we have to trick our brain since all these brain waves lay below our 20 Hz lower hearing range.

For our brains to have Hemispheric Synchronization occur the difference of the two tones must not be greater than 30 Hz. Otherwise, the brain perceives the two tones as separate and cannot produce the binaural beat effect.

Binaural Beats are what are known as Standing Waves. A binaural tone is actually a standing wave produced in the brain itself, appearing to be heard in our ears and only possible due to Binaural Hearing.

If we feed one ear a 100hz tone submerged in white noise or music and we feed the other ear perhaps 108hz tone in the other ear, again submerged in white noise or music, the effect is that the two hemispheres of the brain are resonating at different rates, but between the hemispheres there is a beat of 8hz which will effectively put you in an Alpha state, perfect for meditation of the sort we desire for Divining and Active Magickal practices.

Quieting the Mind, a Practical Approach

First off, if you do a web search for 'meditation steps' or 'How to Meditate' you'll most likely get hammered with advertisement after advertisement pitching either a meditation course or a guided meditation CD.

First, I do not recommend guided meditation CDs. They can become a crutch and be a problem later. You really need to learn to meditate on your own.

For Magickal Adepts I recommend the organic time-tested traditional meditation techniques at first. Then, moving on to a modern Binaural Beats technology.

To start I simply recommend spending two to five minutes a day being quiet and alone with your thoughts. When I first started, I'd close my office door after lunch for a couple of minutes.

It was easy! I'd sit in my office chair, both feet on the floor, my arms relaxed and my hands on my knees. Then I reached over, and I started an inexpensive kitchen timer set to 2 minutes on my desk. I closed my eyes, took slow deep breaths, and blew them out slowly in a puckered lips mode. When the timer began to beep, I simply turned it off and got on with my afternoon office chores.

I made every effort to do it every day as I returned from lunch. That's the hard part, keeping the daily routine going. After a couple of months, I realized I wanted a little bit more quiet time. So, the next day I set the timer for three minutes. I did three minutes a day for another couple of months. Then I added another minute. When I reached five minutes several months later, I started an evening meditation session at home just before bedtime, with approximately the same five-minute period. This routine gave me about ten minutes a day of meditative quietness.

If I decided to do a magickal working or a divination at home, I followed the same routine of sitting in a straight back chair, feet on the ground with breathing. After 5-10 minutes in a meditative state, I would start whatever magickal task I had planned and had setup before meditation.

When I started working with Binaural Beats technology it was a different can of worms. **Read this carefully.** Initially the Binaural Beats so relaxed me I nodded off and fell off the chair. It's not uncommon for beginners to fall asleep when they first experience the intense relaxing that accompanies the initial guided session. Thereafter I began sitting upright on a couch or an over-stuffed chair. If I fell asleep there was little risk of falling out of the chair and hurting myself.

After about a dozen sessions with the Binaural Beats, I was able to keep my focus and not fall asleep. The trick is to maintain a degree of focused awareness. You sort of have to hover between slipping into sleep and being fully alert. Trust me when I say it takes practice and continued effort. But it can be mastered. It just takes practice. Besides, you are a dedicated Magickal Adept, you are in it for the long haul!

When I began to introduce my students, I took another approach. I purchased a headphone distributor. It's a box with a place to plug the CD player into, and there were four or eight output jacks. For health reasons, I had each student purchase their own set of ear covering headphones. Note that I said ear covering. Ear buds don't cut it! The earbuds don't have the acoustic range to properly reproduce the submerged tones in the ocean wave sounds, white noise or soft music the Binaural Beats CDs used.

With the first few student sessions, I would have them all lie down on the floor on yoga mats. After I started the Binaural Beats CD, they all relaxed and were all snoring within 5-12 minutes. The guided session runs about 30 minutes so I would just let them all sleep. Then in the last 5-8 minutes of the CD program, there are rhythmic waking tones that sort of sound like someone dragging their fingers over the teeth of a comb. Yes, it's annoying but it brings you back to consciousness. If they were truly meditating most people would just ease back to consciousness. If they were sleeping, it was a bit jarring and woke them up rather abruptly. After three or perhaps four sessions most students are able to maintain a meditative focus through the session.

That said, I have had a couple of students who always fell asleep with the Binaural Beats CDs. I had them focus on mastering their breathing and walking meditation instead.

So why do this type of meditation? After you have been working with the Binaural Beats CDs, most people find it a lot easier to meditate on their own. The concept works like this. Once you really have been in the ideal meditative zone, you will know what you are trying to achieve with sitting meditation.

There are a lot of these Binaural Beats CDs on the market. I strongly recommend the Hemi-Sync™ technology. Available from: **https://hemi-sync.com** and from **https://monroeinstitute.org**

Practicing Active Magick – Mental Imagery

Every night I lie in bed
The brightest colors fill my head
A million dreams are keeping me awake
A million dreams, a million dreams
I think of what the world could be
A vision of the one I see
A million dreams is all its gonna take
A million dreams for the world we're gonna make.

"A Million Dreams" from The Greatest Showman

Written By Benj Pasek & Justin Paul

When practicing active magic using the visualization method, it's important to consider the active method of spell delivery. How often we hear some practitioners relate an account of a circle practice of 5 to 25 or more persons. We hear a statement like, *"oh we raised some great energy!"*

My humble opinion of this statement is that they didn't raise energy. But rather got everyone pumped up with a chanting ritual and at its peak, the group had an endorphin rush. Now I know that previous statement is going to get me verbally crucified. Yes, they may have generated magical output. Hopefully, everyone involved was focused on the same intention. But statistically speaking, they probably weren't.

Point one: For the record, it is very hard to get a collection of individuals, all focused on the same target intention.

Point two: There is this belief that one grand application of magical intention is best. The idea, I suppose, is conceptually to make one loud request. With many voices crying out in unison. Still others tell me that it is like a big blast of a fire hose full of intention.

Bottom line: "their view is bigger, grander; loudness is better"

My position, "It is NOT!" This Rogue Witch comes from the magickal school of thought that good magic is as gentle as a baby's breath. In essence, perhaps it is better to project 100 or perhaps a thousand, little heart felt, well focused visualizations of intention versus one big loud one.

Metaphor: I can swing a sledgehammer at a huge block of ice and maybe I'll break it in half but most likely I won't. On the other hand, I might have more success gently hitting it multiple times with a small pickax and after 10, 20, 30 or perhaps 50 times I'll just hit the right flaw and shatter the block of ice.

For many years when I really wanted to manifest something, I practiced a daily routine of short, focused thought projections towards the desired intention. Sometimes this was done daily for a few weeks. Sometimes daily for many months. In a few cases, daily for perhaps a year or more.

In many cases the magick for the causes to make the desired thing manifest eventually came to pass. Sometimes exactly the way I visualized it! Sometimes it came in the form of a door being opened that allowed the manifestation to occur through more mundane efforts and methods. But in all cases the manifestation occurred.

The key was small, regular, focused thought projections repeatedly done on a daily basis for as long as it took. All things considered, sometimes the manifestation occurred but wasn't what I wanted, but rather what I needed. The lesson here is "the force knows best!"

With regards to those little bursts of focused magickal thought, in essence, tiny nudges. The question is often asked of me: Were those little rituals of a sort? The answer is complicated. It's both. Yes and no. But in each case, there were no herbs, no candles, no crystals, no incense, and no invocations of Gods and Goddesses.

They were simply acts of clearing my mind and focusing my visual thoughts on the desired intention, for perhaps two to five minutes a day, every day over long periods of time. There's no need to raise great powerful force. Just be gently persistent.

Naturally, I can hear some of you saying, *"But I can't wait weeks, months, or years for my spell to manifest."*

Magick is not like the pizza place, *get your magickal manifestation in 30 minutes or less.* Magick doesn't work like that, get used to it! My only consoling thoughts are that all things come in their own time and season.

Sometimes big wishes and colossal manifestations come quickly if karma is with you! Sometimes they take quite a while. In some cases, they seemingly don't come at all. Then one day several years after your casting, wham! bam! It manifests when you least expect it. When this long-delayed manifestation occurs, all you can do is suck it up, ride the wave and roll with it. And oh, my, yes you will find yourself scrambling to keep up.

Does magical manifestation really work? Yes, it most certainly does. But magick isn't a tool you use routinely. In addition, there are practical limits. Don't ask to be a great rock music star if you don't play an instrument. Don't ask to be a glamorous movie star if you've never been in a play or had acting lessons. Don't ask to be a brain surgeon if you haven't been to medical school. The lesson I have preached for three decades: Do all the mundane aspects of that thing you want to be first! Then consider using magickal means to get a door opened.

Story Time

I knew a talented musician gal once who did this huge ritual to initiate a wish for her musical recording career to take off. She wished for 10 hit albums and money. The problem here is the literal aspect of magick. Wishing for a specific thing; versus the causes for the path for the eventual outcome.

What's remarkable was that a few weeks later someone gave her 10 CDs of hit artists. Likewise, about the same month, she received a significant dividend check from her insurance company quite unexpectedly. From my point of view, her spell worked precisely as specified. This is clearly an example of the principle of literal magic. In magick, specifications are everything.

If you are an artist, it's essential to do all the hard work of honing your skill in the desired profession or vocation. Magick comes into play when you're trying to get a break. The break might be an audition with an agent. It might be a job interview with a producer. It might merely be an appointment with an influential person in your particular profession.

Here's an example: I know a performance artist who had put together this really good comedy standup act. She tried for weeks and months to get an appointment with an agent who dealt with standup comics, but she couldn't get past the battle-hardened secretary in his office.

She worked a ritual to get an appointment, just an appointment to pitch her act. The next day she made another attempt to make a telephone call for an appointment. As luck or magick would have it, the secretary was out running errands, and the agent himself answered his own phone.

She pitched herself and landed an appointment. The agent liked her material but told her he couldn't use her. The comic in question went home rejected but happy that she'd gotten an appointment for the audition. When the comic got home, there was a voicemail waiting. It turned out to be from a colleague of the agent. While the agent she auditioned for couldn't use her, he put in a good word about her with his colleague. Who in turn arranged for another audition for her to show her stuff, and she landed a comedy circuit booking. This is magick at its best!

Another example: Back in the late 1980s and early 1990s, I was trying to get a cable television show about Witchcraft launched. You must understand that in that era, the public's view of witchcraft was still very much "It's all black magic and witches are bad people."

I approached several cable access television stations with a proposal for me to produce a cable series about what real witchcraft was about. Time after time, I got doors slammed in my face. Finally, with humility and conviction, I pitched the president of a small cable station in Virginia.

It was a hard sell, but at least she listened to me. She had considerable reservations but gave me a small contract for a measly six episodes as a summer replacement program. If I had stomped away in a hissy-fit, I suspect that I would have probably never gotten the chance to tell the witchcraft story. I smiled and happily signed the six-episode contract.

The following weekend, I assembled a magickal content team. We put a turkey in the oven, and I polled the team for program topic ideas. The concept was simple: "everything was up for grabs." This exercise generated a list of nearly eighty program ideas. Then by consensus we ranked them. This next exercise went like this, I have a contract for six programs. Which ones do we do first? The six people discussed the pros and cons of the various topics and ranked what they thought should be done first. Of course, they all kept telling me that the cable station would probably air the first program and an anti-witch public outcry would cancel the rest of the shows. But I told them to imagine that we'd get additional contracts. With that we proceeded to rank the rest of the show ideas. By the time the turkey dinner was ready, we'd ranked all eighty of the program ideas.

If you read what I just said, you can see that for four hours, I got six people to imagine and visualize about 80 programs about magick and the craft community. This is another way of generating group magick.

I assembled a television production team, and over the next few springtime months, we taped the six episodes for future play sometime during the summer. A couple of weeks after we had wrapped up taping, a lady came to my door and told me that I needed to call the cable station because something had happened.

I didn't have a phone at the time, so I walked to a convenience store and used a payphone to call the station. The station's staff producer told me that a 300-word Associated Press story had gone out on the wires earlier in the day about my as yet untelevised program. I asked him what the problem was. That's when he told me that CBS and ABC news were sitting in the lobby, and they wanted to talk to the Witches!

Suddenly and inexplicably, national and international media visibility was raining down upon the obscure little Virginia cable station. In the weeks that followed, the cable station's president gave me a pair of thirteen-week contracts to continue producing the witchcraft-oriented program. Over the next two years, we received additional contracts, as well as an award for television excellence.

Ultimately, we produced seventy, thirty-minute witchcraft television talk shows. The host and I granted nearly a hundred domestic and international, press, tv and radio interviews over the two-year time frame of the program. All done with the focused intention of helping to change the negative narrative and image of witchcraft.

My television production team and I were all talented television people, and we all knew our trade, this was the mundane aspect. As well my magickal content team were all seasoned practitioners and socially connected and knew just about everybody we'd need as subject matter experts for each of the programs.

My applied magickal kick in the pants was a magickal working for "media visibility," which was performed on the holiday of Ostara, a classic fertility holiday and rite. Again, this was magick at its best!

Let's fast forward twenty years to 2013. I had retired from an aerospace career with a huge military defense contractor. After retiring, I enrolled in college to complete a long overdue degree in entertainment writing. During my degree studies I developed an interest in UFO sightings stories. I decided to write some blog-column articles about UFO activity in New York State, where I lived. I pitched Newspaper editors at a variety of daily newspapers. One after another they turned me down and, in a few cases, they literally laughed me out of their offices telling me the subject matter was ludicrous.

After each time that I was turned down, I did one of my ritual meditation sessions. After a few more rejections, I humbly reached out to a small weekly newspaper as a last resort. Again, in my meditation session I projected the notion of getting a break and being given a trial period for a few weeks. Had I walked away after a half dozen rejections from the big upstate newspapers, my project would not have gone anywhere.

Finally, I had a chat with the editor at the weekly newspaper, and I pitched my proposal. The editor was interested and told me he'd try me out for a month. A month later, he asked me to come over to chat. When I heard from him, I figured the trial period was over and that he was letting me go. At the meeting he told me to keep doing what I was doing, that my blog-column was a hit with readers. A few months later, the editor published a page two story, that the most popular column at the newspaper wasn't in print but carried on their online edition. Shortly after that the digital services editor who managed the web edition called me and told me I now had a national audience and to keep up the good work. Months after that, at the Christmas party, the editors told me I was drawing a significant international readership as well.

That blog column had 237 published columns, ran for seven years and garnered international recognition and a **Researcher of the Year** award. As of this writing in the summer of 2021, several streaming television series are in the works based upon my writing and research.

LESSON 1: Make sure you are skilled in the thing you are pursuing, be humble, be patient and gently keep impressing that wish imagery to the younger self during your clear-headed meditation sessions.

LESSON 2: Develop your skill at visualizing the situation you want. Picture yourself dealing with the high points and low points of working in that particular situation. Think of it like a magickal daydream.

Finally, take the time to meditate a little every day. Make a serious effort to learn how to quiet your mind in order to make room for clear visualization and imagining!

Practicing Active Magick – Blind Targets

This essay is about benevolent blind magick. In other words, working magick for everybody else vs. yourself. The mechanism is a simple correspondence magickal principle.

Preparation: It works like this. You write out a pile of simple 3x5 cards with very specific wishes for health and/or prosperity for a specific person or group of people you know. Possibly a group of people you don't know. Perhaps the population of a struggling village somewhere. After you write out these cards, you stuff and seal them individually into unlabeled security envelopes.

After stuffing these many envelopes, you shuffle them up and a few days later get on your computer and assign an eight-to-twelve-digit random number or random alpha numeric sequence on the outside of each. After you label these envelopes, you put them in a small box or tub or perhaps a cloth sack.

I recommend initially preparing perhaps thirty to fifty envelopes. Then each week make it a discipline to add five additional stuffed envelopes with new random sequences.

Then perhaps once per week schedule yourself a special benevolence meditation session as a magickal working. Prior to starting that session reach deep into the box or bag where you store these envelopes and withdraw one.

Then sit down, quiet yourself. After getting quiet of mind, focus your attention on the number sequence on the envelope you withdrew.

Repeat the number sequence over and over again in your quiet mind, whisper it if need be. Think of this number sequence as a mantra of sorts. In your mind offer thoughts of peace, joy, welcoming, abundance and gentle positive loving kindness. I recommend a 5 to 10-minute meditation if you are up to it. Think of this weekly offering as a repayment to the universe for the good things and abundance that have come into your life.

Please keep this a positive and benevolent exercise. Remember: NO attack magick or whammy intentions. Remember this meditative working is about everybody else and not you!

I can hear some of you thinking or muttering. *"Why am I going to waste my time doing a weekly benevolent exercise for a whole pile of strangers I don't know?"*

As I stated in a previous chapter, it's simple: ***"With great power comes great responsibility"***

You as a magickal adept have unique talents and have developed wonderfully powerful skills. We as magickal adepts have a responsibility to make reality a better place for everybody. Consider all the problems our Earth-bound human family suffers day to day. Your efforts will be felt.

Repetition in Magickal Castings

My experience has been that all workings really should be given multiple castings. We don't drive a nail into a board with one swing of the hammer. The effort takes many taps of the hammer to drive the nail into position.

In terms of a Magickal working there are several good reasons for multiple castings for the same intent.

> 1: To refine your intent. After all, <u>Intention is everything in magick</u>.
>
> 2: Multiple castings will increase the weight of your desire for the intention to manifest.

Some traditions of Craft practice suggest that you do a spell casting at least three times. I couldn't agree more when it comes to routine day-to-day magickal castings.

Degrees of Magickal Effort and Effect

Some Magickal writers use the term to "Bend or Manipulate" reality in the process of doing a magickal working. But let's look at some preciseness in our language. What we're actually doing in terms of degrees of magickal effort and effect.

If we **<u>Impress</u>** <u>upon reality</u>, we are perhaps briefly putting a **Dimple** into the fabric of it for all intents and purposes. Reality is stubbornly persistent as Albert Einstein once said. In this case, the fabric of reality readily bounces back after a magickal effort. Much like pressing on a rubber ball that instantly returns to its normal form after the pressure of the Impress is released. This is typically the result associated with day-to-day castings and other forms of casual magickal workings.

If we **Bend** reality, we are perhaps making a more pronounced change to the fabric for all intents and purposes. As I said previously Reality is stubbornly persistent, in this case the fabric of reality will again bounce back after a magickal effort, but much like an older soft foam pillow, it will bounce back a bit more slowly after we impress upon it. This is typically the result of longer term repeated small magickal workings over a short period of time, perhaps many weeks or months.

If we **Fold** reality, we are perhaps making a more significant change to the fabric. This is typically the result of longer-term efforts over many years of resolute magickal workings on a very focused intent. With this sort of change to reality, the fabric would be less resilient and perhaps our impress will be more semi-permanent in nature. Werner Heisenberg's uncertainty principle applies here. This kind of mystical effort results in reality never quite being the same again after it bounces back. This sort of magickal working is very much in the realm of seasoned, committed and focused mystics and magickal practitioners.

If we **Warp** reality, we are making a significant change to reality's fabric. This typically is the result of extremely long term-perhaps over decades-efforts and relentless heavy duty magickal workings. The result is a catastrophic alteration in the fabric, where reality's structure is irreparably changed and permanent. Again, this sort of magickal working is without a doubt exclusively in the domain of the dedicated, committed and focused mystical practitioners.

Practice Magick Ever So Gently

Words and the thoughts behind them are potent. As a teacher to new students, one must be careful how you think of things in your mind and speak softly with words that call about change and manipulation of matters.

Have you ever seen a mobile made from Dominoes? One flick of a finger sets off a chain reaction that usually grows bigger and bigger.

While I was in the military, I learned the saying or a story:

> For the want of a nail, a shoe was lost.
> For the want of a shoe, a horse was lost.
> For the want of a horse, a rider was lost.
> For the want of a rider, a message was lost.
> For the want of a message, a battle was lost.
> For the want of a battle, a kingdom was lost.
> And all for the want of a horseshoe nail.

How often do we hear news of the train wreck or car accident that was caused by a malfunction of a part that costs less than a couple of dollars?

Magick is always about cause and effect. If you can "massage the causes," you can manipulate the resulting effect.

For years I have watched apprentice practitioners try to produce a magickal effect; bright, loud, and full of whiz-bang-- like the special CGI effects we see in the movies. I've tried to caution these students against what they are doing. But I used to get dismissed as a busybody. These days I get blown off as a crazy old fool.

Please respect the wisdom and experience of elders, use magic ever so gently!

I will teach you magick with informed consent. If you screw up, it's on you. I warned you!

This is the: "I told you so, clause."

My eldest daughter, a seasoned adept, read a narrative I wrote about magick that I wrote two decades ago. She complained that I explained the magickal process so well that just about anybody could understand it. That's when she objected in no uncertain terms that I was giving away the store.

"You're passing out loaded shotguns to third graders," she said metaphorically.

I sat on the manuscript for a dozen years, then reread it, and after doing so, I took it in the back yard and poured charcoal lighter fluid on it and burned it.

Karma is an absolute law of the universe. I know a lot of witches and pagans who don't believe in karma. I console them, and I reassure them that karma believes in them.

If I teach you serious-minded magick, you run the risk of seriously screwing up. Because I showed you, I personally run the risk of karmic backlash, the likes of which you cannot imagine. Therefore, I require my students to assume full responsibility for the magick they work.

You come to magick of your own free will. By this commitment and this reckoning, you also assume full responsibility for your magickal practice.

If you can't accept the responsibility, then it's simple:

DON'T PRACTICE MAGICK!

Don't whine about what you screwed up, suck it up and fix it.

There's an old computer systems adage:

"To err is human; to really foul things up requires a computer."

In magical terms the adage goes like this:

"To err is human; to mess things up on an exponential scale requires badly executed magick."

A beginning student typically has this notion that magick is supposed to have bright flashes and whiz-bangs like they see in the movies.

Real magick, properly executed is as gentle as a baby's breath, merely a gentle nudge.

If you do a magickal working, you should observe what the result is, as opposed to what was intended. If you messed up, fix it. Notice I did not say if the result isn't to your liking. Big difference

Example: I knew a witch in upstate New York who had a major jerk of a boss. So, the witch figured he'd get his boss transferred to an out-of-state location. The working was successful. The boss was transferred to the mid-Atlantic HQ of the business. But in our age of global Internet connectivity, the jerk boss remained the manager of the upstate New York branch managing old New York folks from Baltimore. Plus, he picked up the responsibility for a similar function at several other facilities. In the end, the witch still had the same boss, but the boss was just out of the state.

The magick worked perfectly, except that karma continued the relationship, so what is the lesson here?

There is sloppy magick, and there is good magick. There is also karma, which is potentially capable of undermining good or bad magick; trust me, it frequently does. I have observed over the years that if karma is at the root of any significant variation in your magickal working, you won't be able to change the situation, no matter what. End of story!

Finally, as always, be careful and mindful of what you ask for.

Be careful what you ask for...you probably will get it… eventually.

There's a saying in magick; "All things happen in their own time and season."

Many magickal practitioners I've known never pay much mind to the effects of karma, as I stated previously. Nor do they pay attention to the temporal considerations. Temporal considerations, I've found, are a huge deal.

I'll use the example of remote viewing. It was discovered early on that if temporal specifications were not defined on the target card that the individual remote viewers on an away team would find themselves reporting data about the target site from different periods.

There's a classic example of an Army remote viewer reporting data on a Russian base during the cold war. He drew a sketch of the site with high accuracy. The intelligence agency who requested the RV session criticized the session's data because they had aerial photographs that did not show a particular man-made feature that the viewer reported.

As it turned out, two things were discovered: 1: the target card didn't have any time specifications. 2: the man-made feature in contention was built two months later and showed up on later intelligence photographs exactly as the remote viewer had illustrated it.

But let's say you specify a precise time that you want your magick to be effective. The other thing you really must consider is karma. The effects of karma frequently are a huge issue, as I have previously stated.

Karma can and does impact magickal workings. That's not to say that what you were trying to accomplish won't happen. It's just going to happen when the karma ripens enough to allow all the causes to occur.

So, keep in mind: Temporal/time and Karmic considerations when planning a working.

My last thoughts on the topic of temporal and karmic considerations.

I've chatted with practitioners who have sniffed at me when I try to teach this subject at Craft Gatherings. I usually hear a remark like: "Well, my kind of magick always works and is never impeded by anything."

To that remark, I say, "My 44-year viewpoint suggests otherwise."

There's no "little bit of working magick." If you're in for a dime, you're in for a dollar.

If you want to do some protection around your home or bedroom with a little sage and sea salt, that's fine. If you're going to put $5 under the Virgin Mary or your Goddess statue for increased prosperity, that's fine. But the moment you consider performing a working, something that requires spell casting, it's an entirely different story.

I come from the school of thinking that "dabbling" without a commitment to the art of magick only leads to problems. If you don't make the commitment to clearly learn the mechanics of magick, you shouldn't be doing it. I'm not asking you to train up to be a world-class mage; I'm only saying that you need to make some commitment to clearly learn the basics and intermediate elements at the level at which you'll be practicing. Do not practice outside the bounds of your training!

How often do we hear non-magickal people say, "Oh... you shouldn't be messing around with that magick stuff?"

Why do they say that?

Either they did something and did it very wrong, or they knew somebody else who did something magickally and screwed up royally.

The scenario usually goes like this, somebody needed something outside of the realm of mundane resources, so they got the idea that magick might be a solution. They went out and bought a book about spell casting and decided to solve their problem with a splash of homebrew magick.

It's like a first timer trying to make a loaf of bread. The beginner doesn't understand the subtle aspects of the ingredients or working the dough. They make compromises in the process, and the result is usually disastrous or at the very least disappointing. Also, this person's failure only serves to give the magickal practice a bad name.

If you are going to work magick, take the time to study up a bit and don't just sit down with a spell book and dabble. You are only asking for trouble! Consider yourself warned.

That said, if you study up a bit, always work within the boundaries of what you know. It's ok to explore and advance your skills but take the time to study the next level of magick upon which you are planning to embark.

Lastly, learn to meditate, divine, and connect to the great consciousness. I've found that solutions come to you in meditation. It's wisdom that usually doesn't show up in popular books.

"Magickal students learn best when their cell phones are off or locked in their car."

Long ago, 25-30 years ago, we used to unplug the phones and turn on the answering machines in another room, not within earshot of where we were holding our circle.

These days everyone walks around with cell phones in their pockets and purses. The problem, as I see it, is that when people are asked to silence their phones at movies, presentations, or classes, there are always some fools who think the silencing request doesn't apply to them. So, at a tender moment, or an intriguing discourse, someone's phone rings, usually with the most obnoxious ring tone.

Then there is the texting, with the related buzzing and ringing bells. I have sat in a temple prayer room and had my meditation interrupted by others in the quiet space when their phones abruptly rang loudly or buzzed rattling on the prayer benches.

I've watched students sitting on meditation pillows in a perfect lotus position, suddenly open their eyes and pull out their phones from a pocket beneath them. The whole scene looked like they were sitting on a nest trying to hatch something. In any case, they disturbed me and twenty or thirty others who were working at being at peace and one with the universe.

I think what pains me is that if you quietly speak to them about the rules of no phones in the prayer room or in class, they get all indignant or have a hissy fit. Most students apologized and complied. Some students have stomped out; others had to be asked to leave.

When I lived in the Washington, DC area, my questions about the phone justification in the temple or circle space went like this:

Are you part of the White House West Wing Staff? (I have had friends and students who were.)

Are you in the National Security Community and on-call? (I have had students who were.)

Are you a physician or emergency room person on-call? (I have had students who were.)

Are you a volunteer fire-rescue person on-call? (Been there and I have the Fire dept uniform.)

If you are none of these, turn off your phone or lock up your phone in your car for the duration of your temple visit or circle working.

Here's the bottom line:

"You're not going to become an magickal adept, a good witch, a mystical mage or Jedi knight with a cell phone going off every five minutes in your pocket. So, turn off the phone completely, or lock it up in your car. Then come in and contemplate the secrets of the universe."

Part Four-Advanced Magickal Theory

Are Pagan Holidays – Simply a Clock?

Catholic School Teaching

50 plus years ago when I was a good Catholic kid, the nuns taught us to observe the hours of the Angelus. The local church bells would ring at 6am, Noon, and 6pm. At these times we were supposed to stop what we are doing and observe a few minutes of prayer in the form of Three Hail Mary's. I left the Catholic tradition at age 18 and embraced Wicca in 1977 in my mid 20's. To be honest, I never gave the Angelus another thought until recently while doing some metaphysical research to teach an advanced class.

In the pagan tradition, we've been told our Sabbats are astronomical alignments with which to measure the seasons. Also, mainstream science has told us for years that ancient archeological sites that align with the various season sunrises were merely used for agricultural purposes.

The question I asked was: What if there is something more behind these ancient archeological astronomical sites?

Okay, first some Technical History and Science background that has a bearing on this discussion.

The Hunt for Shortwave Noise

In the mid to late 1920s, the Bell telephone company was having serious trouble with their shortwave radio links for trans-oceanic phone calls. The short-wave radio bands they were using were being plagued by severe static interference at various times of the day and night, at never precisely the same time. Bell Labs hired a young physicist and radio engineer from Oklahoma to study the problem, his name was **Karl Guthe Jansky**.

Jansky with his 20.5 MHz antenna.

Jansky built a large wooden frame structure on which to mount a short-wave antenna. He even installed the sizable structure on Model T Ford tires so he could rotate the antenna in a directional search manner. During his study efforts, Jansky made a significant observation. He noted that the static peaked about four minutes earlier every day. In reality, the radio noise was functioning within a 23-hour 56-minute period, and the noise was approximately 4 minutes earlier every day.

After much testing, Jansky realized that the source of the static wasn't coming from any Earthly source; but rather that it was coming from the sky. Later the problem of high levels of radio noise was traced to the Milky Way galaxy passing overhead every **23 hours 56 minutes**. This observation by Jansky in 1931 was an exact correspondence to "star-time" or **sidereal time**. Karl Jansky is considered to be the father of Radio Astronomy. (NOTE: 23h56 mins NOT 24 hrs.)

The 13:30 LST Effect

Sixty-six years later in 1997, a researcher working for the Cognitive Sciences Laboratory in Palo Alto, CA made another substantial discovery that also related to sidereal time. It should be noted that the Cognitive Sciences Laboratory is a descendant of the two-and-a-half-decade-long military Remote Viewing program, which terminated in 1995.

James Spottiswood is an accomplished and classically trained physicist. Spottiswood decided to use a pragmatic approach to measuring the ESP cognition. He wasn't interested in what the ESP experiments were measuring. Instead, the physicist focused on examining any compelling correlation. Using data from 1468 published trials, Spottiswood discovered that no matter what the experiments were measuring, specific tests had a significant "effect size" when the **Local Sidereal Time** was about 13:30 LST. His amazing finding was that within 30 minutes either side of 13:30 LST the "effect size" was four times baseline, in other words, the ESP "effect size" was about 450%. He further observed that within an hour either way of 13:30 LST there ESP "effect size" doubled. What does this mean? Within the two hours centered on 13:30 LST, there is a 200% to 450% increase in the ESP effect size.

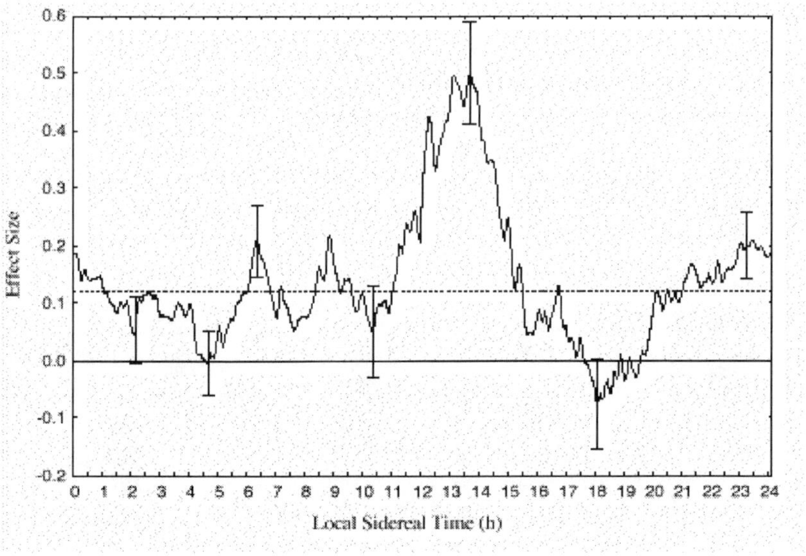

Figure 1- Spottiswood's Chart

As Spottiswood was a traditionally trained scientist, he had to consider the possibility that these preliminary numbers were a fluke. So, he decided to start over again and test his findings, in effect conduct a validation test. He collected another 1015 trials from a range of ESP experiments. Still, the peak magnitude of his second test series confirmed the same time results of **13:30 LST**.

He would later tell a science journal reporter, ***"There's a 24-hour correlation...Don't ask me what it is, but it's real."***

Suddenly the story was out in the media, that ESP now had a "measurable effect" and there was traditional science to back it up. The problem was that most mainstream media at the time just didn't "get it."

All the news reports I read at the time quickly figured out that the Milky Way Galaxy wasn't overhead or high in the sky. The collective media wisdom at the time was that there had to be something like the galaxy overhead beaming down some great power that imbues us humans with increased ESP powers. Nope, the galaxy was on the horizon, nothing was overhead except the constellation Virgo. Everybody just blew it off because there wasn't a simple and obvious causality. Of course, there were some outlandish theories that I will not discuss. In any case, the news cycle quickly faded on this story.

Nevertheless, there was now a measurable ESP effect, but also there was now another unknown. Now for my Wiccan and Mystical readers, ESP in this context translates to Divining and active Magickal workings.

SO, WHAT was the cause? This was the big question.

In late 1998 I was living and studying in a Buddhist Monastery. One of my monastic brothers was an amateur optical astronomer; I was into amateur radio telescope work. One night after discussing Spottiswood's discovery, we sat down with our laptops and handheld Planispheres and started seriously looking at the sky.

After many hours of analysis, we came to two conclusions.

- **First** – The arms of the galaxy were unmistakably on the horizon and <u>not overhead</u>.

- **Second** – All the high-intensity radio noise that Karl Jansky discovered when the galaxy was overhead was <u>more or less absent or minimal</u> during the two-hour window of the 13:30 "ESP effect."

With this realization, my monk friend remarked, *"The 13:30 effect is not about some celestial body imbuing some psychic ability, but rather, it's about the absence of radio frequency noise. It's all about* ***THE QUIET!****"*

Getting back to metaphysics, how does this have an impact on divining and magickal practitioners?

I hear some folks saying, "but this consciousness stuff is all ethereal and shouldn't be affected by radio noise from the galaxy." I agree with that notion, the "part of us" that is spiritually connected to all living things everywhere and everywhen within the multiverse shouldn't be affected by high levels of electromagnetic radio noise from the galaxy.

But consider that we are also biological creatures with senses and electrical impulses that meander within our brains and course throughout our bodies. It's this physical electrical aspect of our bodies that is profoundly affected by the electromagnetic radio noise from the galaxy.

Think of it like this. It's no different from going to a noisy dance club and trying to meditate. The loud noise and physical activity would be a challenge for even a seasoned monastic or mystic trying to get centered. In our 13:30 consideration, high radio noise would physically disrupt our ability to hear the gentle whisper of the **Great Consciousness**.

The Ancient Aliens Connection

A few years back on an **Ancient Aliens** program episode, one of the hosts Giorgio A. Tsoukalos was talking about an ancient site in Turkey. At this site, the king who financed the shrine used to crawl into a special freehold in the early morning hours of **Winter Solstice.** The shaft of this particular cavity would light up with the bright sunlight at sunrise. It is said that the king used that chamber to receive wisdom from the Gods. We also have similar stories from other parts of the world. In the temple at Karnack, Egypt a specific chamber lights up around sunrise. The statuary in the temple shows the Pharaoh sitting with the Egyptian Gods on either side of him.

I did a bit of further research and the **Winter Solstice** sunrise and early morning period seem to be a significant driving theme with most of these ancient sites.

On several other **Ancient Aliens** programs, host Andrew Collins made a significant point about the Constellation Cygnus (the Northern Cross) being a big deal with ancient peoples.

My Hypothesis

I suspected that these ancient sites were more than just agricultural season markers as mainstream science has suggested. What if these sites were designed to mark the window time of the 13:30 LST effect? In essence, a sky clock of sorts, intended to show ancient people when they could mystically touch the **Great Consciousness** of the Universe?

The Paper Experiment

Newgrange a Stone Age (Neolithic) monument in the Boyne Valley, County Meath (Ireland) is 5200 years old (3,200 B.C.). Newgrange is best known for the illumination of its passage-chamber by the winter solstice sun. Above the entrance to the passage-chamber at Newgrange, there is an opening called a roof-box. This baffling orifice held a great surprise for those who unearthed it. Its purpose is to allow sunlight to penetrate the chamber on the shortest days of the year, around December 21st, the winter solstice. At dawn, from December 19th to 23rd, a narrow beam of light penetrates the roof-box and reaches the floor of the chamber, gradually extending to the rear of the chamber.

As the sun rises higher, the beam widens within the chamber so that the whole room becomes dramatically illuminated. This event lasts for 17 minutes, beginning around 9 AM. The accuracy of Newgrange as a time-telling device is remarkable when one considers that it was built 500 years before the Great Pyramids and more than 1,000 years before Stonehenge.

I conducted a paper analysis, I looked up the latitude and longitude of the site and the local time reference. Then performed a calculation to determine if the two hours of the 13:30 LST effect window would occur between 7am and 9am local time.

If one were to celebrate a mystical ritual starting at 7am on the three days of Winter Solstice, they would be rewarded with the light up of the chamber effect at the end of their ceremony.

How would they know when to start the ritual? Easy, with the rising and setting of certain constellations in the pre-dawn sky! **Orion had just set, and Cygnus is rising.** When would they finish the ritual period? At **Sunrise!**

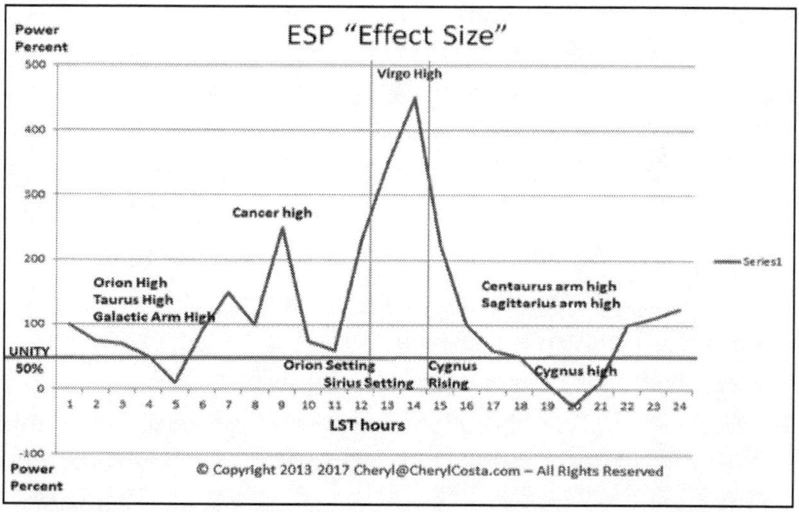

The KEY to this whole process is "THE GALACTIC QUIET!"

Remember sidereal time isn't the same every day. It's approximately 4 minutes earlier each day. So, it's ever moving. Needless to say, our ancestors needed nighttime and daytime rules and tools to know when to touch the Great Consciousness.

We in modern times can web search LST calculators and compute the proper time for the two hours "LST ESP EFFECT Window" anytime we want to. But our ancient predecessors didn't have the precision clocks, but they did have the sky at night and the rising and setting of various constellations as well as the movements of the sun.

Whoever taught our forefathers and foremothers the secret of the best time of day to do mystical rituals must have used the sky as a clock. But some of the best times happen during the daylight hours, so the ancients built astronomical calculators with stone structures all over the world. Some only measure the Winter Solstice. Others display measurements at other times of the day at different times of the year. Interestingly, some of the times nicely line up with the traditional Catholic Angelus times. Hmmm…

Sabbat	Date	12:30 LST	13:30 LST	14:30 LST
Samhain	31-Oct	11:00am	Noon	1:00pm
Yule	21-Dec	6:37am	7:37am	8:37am
Imbolc	2-Feb	3:39am	4:49am	5:49am
Ostara	21-Mar	1:43am	2:43am	3:43am
Beltane	1-May	11:00pm	Midnight	1:00am
Litha	21-Jun	7:39pm	8:39pm	9:39pm
Lammas	1-Aug	4:56pm	5:56pm	6:56pm
Mabon	21-Sep	1:37am	2:37am	3:37am
	Magickal Yield Increase	250%	400%	250%

Sidereal time is dependent on your local Latitude and most importantly your longitude. The chart above of LST window times below is based on sidereal time calculations for where I used to live in **Syracuse, NY** (**DMS Long**: 76° 9' 16.1280" W -- **DMS Lat**: 43° 5' 20.2092."

Sunrise on 21 Dec Winter Solstice is roughly 13:30 LST locally. Likewise, **Sunset** on 21 June is approximately 13:30 LST locally.

13:30 Effect-How to use it

After that whole big write up about the 13:30 LST effect, I've had many a witchlet, seasoned witch, and venerable mystic grouse at me that they aren't getting up in the middle of the night to do a divining meditation or do a magickal working.

It is important to note that in six months of the year the 13:30 LST window is during the overnight hours or other time period not easily compatible with the routine cycle of western daily activity. I'm not saying that every magickal working you do, or divining session should be done within the 13:30 LST window. It's just not practical.

But if you have an unusually important working or an equally important ethereal data mining to accomplish, you might want to plan your schedule to accomplish your important mystical task during the 13:30 LST window.

My advice is to plan for a two-hour period. Do your preparatory cooling down meditation or opening ritual in the 30 minutes before the peak window starts at about 12:30 LST. By the time you are going to be deep into your meditation or your ritual you'll be in the 13:00 to 14:00 peak period.

Many a student has come to me trying to calculate the 13:30 LST precisely, you do not require that sort of precision. All you really need is to be approximately within the window. Keep in mind that our ancestors measured LST times by the rising and setting of the Sun or the rising and setting of certain star constellations.

Of course, in our century, there are apps that function in 23-hour 56-minute days to run on your phones or pads. With a clock like that initially and properly set, you would always know your local sidereal time. A smart mystic would be well advised to download a good LST app for your phone. That said, I am not recommending taking a phone into your mystical space. What I am recommending is if you have such an app, that you use it to figure out when your 13:30 LST window would occur for your local time. That app should only be used for pre-mystical event planning!

Hidden Secrets in Plain Sight

Many times, a mystic or teaching Yogi will say something very silly and seemingly absurd. In the Art of Magick and Mysticism some things are not as they appear, and other things are exactly as they appear and blurt out their secrets for all to hear but are usually misunderstood or simply dismissed as ludicrous.

Case in point. It's often said that some of the best Mystical Secrets are hidden in plain sight. Sometimes in nursery rhymes and many times they are hidden in children's songs. Is the secret of the 13:30 LST effect hidden in children's lore or perhaps popular children's songs? I say, **YES!**

One example is **"When you Wish Upon a Star"** by songwriters Leigh Harline and Ned Washington. The piece was written for Walt Disney's 1940 adaptation of Pinocchio.

Respecting copyright, I can only share a stanza of the lyrics under fair-use-rules. Do a web search for the complete lyrics if you like and listen to a performed version online!

"When you Wish Upon a Star" the song's second stanza is:

"If your heart is in your dream
No request is too extreme
When you wish upon a star
As dreamers do"

Let's do a magickal analysis:

"If your heart is in your dream" - This is a clue to an altered state of consciousness or the meditative dreamy state.

"No request is too extreme" - All the potential of the creative force is at your request!

"When you wish upon a star, As dreamers do." - Make that wish or magickal request under the light of that special star in the dreamy, altered state of waking meditation.

I know some of you are asking, *"But what star?"*

Publicly and mundanely to Wish Upon A Star often refers to making a wish upon seeing the first star in the sky at night. Therein lies the secret of magick protecting itself.

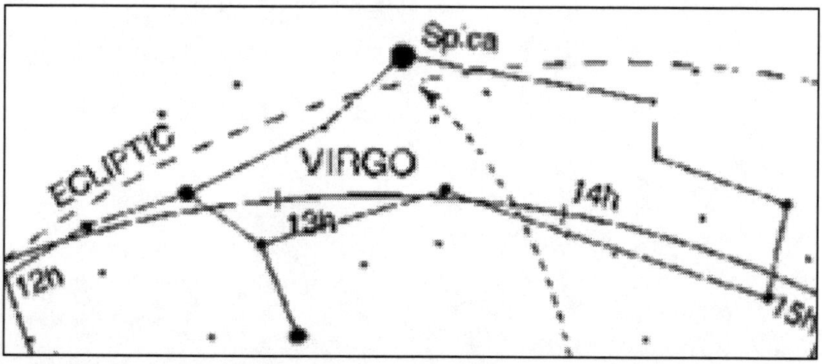

In the song, you are told what to do and how to do it, but not the deeper knowledge of which star.

Elsewhere in mystical works the constellation is called out. Constellation VIRGO is typically described as the Virgin or Queen of all potential. In essence this is the Virgin that has the seeds for Infinite Universes.

We know that the Virgo constellation is high overhead during 13:00 LST and 14:00 LST period. The Star is SPICA at 13:30 LST.

Whether you want to touch deep esoteric knowledge, or perform a masterful magickal work, the 13:30 LST effect is your private channel to the Virgin Queen of Infinite Potential. Use it wisely!

Part Five - Rules of the Road

Recommended Rules of the Magickal Path

These are my recommended Magickal Rules of the road. None of these are hard and fast rules as much as they are a well thought out guideline.

You come to the magickal arts of your own free will.

The scenario goes like this: I'll be sitting in a coffee shop scribbling in my journal narrative, minding my own business. You, whoever you are, approach and ask to speak to me. I invite you to join me in my booth. I offer to buy you a cup of coffee or tea. You tell me you would like to study the magical arts with me. I reply with some questions.

Why do you want to study magick and why are you asking me?

Why magick? It's a question about character. If you want to study for vague reasons, I'll tell you to go home and think it over and come back and see me in a few days. If I hear that you want to influence someone in love and affairs of the heart, I'll give you five dollars and tell you to go buy that special someone a lovely greeting card.

If I hear hostile inclinations, I'll say no and dismiss you

If I hear highly noble reasons, I'll most probably dismiss you too.

I'm not going to tell you what the right answer is!

If you've gotten this far, I'll press you on the question of "why me?" After you've done a great job of trying to flatter me up. I'll tell you I am meaner than the nastiest coach you ever had in high school.

Hopefully, that will convince you that I'm not the teacher for you. Please understand I'm under absolutely no obligation to teach you magick craft, none whatsoever.

If you try to butter me up and appeal to my ego, you're barking up the wrong tree.

You might get my attention if you engage me in a discussion about silly stuff. *"I mean, why do people call it a hot water heater, I mean it's really a cold-water heater, isn't it?"*

If I detect a hint that you think I'm nuts. I will assure you that I'm crazier than the Mad Hatter; and I'll suggest you seek another teacher.

On the other hand, if you dare to go into the silliness realm with me, I'll probably buy you another cup of whatever you are sipping. Why?

Well, you just showed me a degree of flexibility and a willingness to stretch the boundaries of your reality. The bottom line in the world of quantum mechanics and of magick; is that at times, it is seemingly silly, contrary, and very much counter intuitive.

The study of these topics requires your free will. You must choose to do magick not because you were born to it, drafted into it, or ordered to do it, or told to do so under duress. Example: You're only studying magick because your mom, dad, or girlfriend insisted. Wrong answer!

You have to want this for yourself! You have to come to this of your own free will, end of story.

Never bind another person

Of all my student rules, this is the most serious. There's a principle in magic that what you send out, most especially if unjustified, can usually come back upon you threefold. Be warned never bind someone with magic.

Case in point, I knew a man who had a rumor started about him that he was a serious misogynist. I knew him to be a bit awkward around women, and all too often, he said the wrong things, and ladies were frequently very annoyed with him.

One summer, a lady got very outraged at him for making an honest pass at her. Enraged, she ranted to her girlfriends, witches all. And before you know it, all of them were wound up and decided to fix the man's wagon. The five of them went into the woods and did a serious binding spell. The nature of which was that he would never find the love of his life till he changed his ways.

I guess none of these young priestesses had ever heard of pastoral counseling or intervention or perhaps buying the man a cup of coffee and talking to him about his manner. Instead, they chose to be judge, jury, and punisher.

This spell was worked a bit over 30 years ago if my memory serves.

The man in question met the woman of his dreams a year or so later. They were happily married for a bit over 20 years until he had an untimely stroke and passed away.

The five priestesses had success in their careers, but none of them ever found the loves of their lives. Each of them is now a middle-aged spinster. This is what we call in the magical trade a significant magical blowback. Be warned: never bind someone with magick.

Never pray for the demise of your enemies

This goes in the category of "Don't do Hostile Magick!"

1st: Casting against others is against Wiccan Law! It's the Law. (Oh? You're not Wiccan! Then ignore the principle at your own risk.)

2nd: Never do magic in a hostile state of mind or in a hateful fever.

If you do hostile magick, especially in a hateful fever, you risk unintentional collateral damage. If you do hostile magick, you most certainly risk a magickal rebound because you weren't justified, and the universe knows it. Students, remember what I said about magickal blowback.

Working magick in a hateful state of mind is not appropriate and most undoubtedly sloppy. Add to that the overriding ethics issues, namely, "who appointed you judge, jury, and punisher?"

Many of my early magickal teachers recommended that you wait for at least one moon cycle before considering hostile magick. The idea is to give you a chance to cool off and think about your grievance and whether it's worth your time and trouble to attack someone you are just upset with or that you believe did grievous harm to you.

There are many people over the years that have done mean nasty things to me. Since learning the magickal arts, I have refrained from attacking anyone with hostile magick. First, it's mean and second, it's not a fair fight!

Attack magick, right or wrong shouldn't be done in the heat of the moment. But instead, it should be done cooled off, clear of mind, and well thought out. Not to mention well-crafted and well-executed. In other words, attack magick must be premeditated. Am I encouraging this sort of action? Absolutely not!

One of my most excellent teachers preferred the approach of the "nice day wish."

The principal

Wish the jerk a lovely, joyful, abundant day or perhaps an abundant month. Maybe he or she really needs it. If he or she doesn't deserve it, the rebound is happiness for you. But let us consider that what they really needed was a break. A nice day or a nice month might be a positive turning point for them.

On the other hand, if the subject in question is really a dyed in the wool jerk, the universe will abundantly ripen his or her karma, and that will be that.

That is the philosophy for what I call little-fish-hostiles. Let's take a moment to consider the drug cartel lords, the terrorist masterminds, the very public so-called really evil people, the big-fish-hostiles.

Is it your responsibility to take these big bad guys out? In a word, NO! That's karma's responsibility. Get your damned ego out of it! You are not Captain Magick going after the nasties. You are little more than a magickal vigilante, plain and simple.

But what about the really big fish? The Bin Ladens and the Saddam Hussein types and folks like them.

I like the approach of "**No place to hide!**" This is the spell-concept of "No place to hide!"

Incantation theme: "May his/her injustices be dealt with by the greater right of the universe! May his/her sins and karma against humanity be ripened in the light of righteous examination and may he/she find no place to hide from the sins and karma. Bring him/her justice!"

The concept is to ripen the karma of the big fish hostile and bring the power of providence down upon him/her, especially if the authorities of man can't.

{"No place to hide!" Inspired from the 1930s church gospel song by Dorothy Love Coates "No Hiding Place"}

Never use magick to attract money.

You might not like where it comes from.

In the 44 plus years that I've been involved with magick, the most common request that comes from non-magical folks and beginner students is for money spells and love spells.

Money Spells

In my early Catholic upbringing, I saw many traditional household spells, where a dollar or a five-dollar bill was put under the statue of the Virgin Mary. Actually, there's nothing wrong with that method of folk magic. To be honest, it's tried and true. Why?

Explanation: The statue of the Virgin Mary is symbolic of the Great Goddess, and the currency script placed underneath is very visual; therefore, being symbolic both are excellent tools for communicating with the Younger self. In magick, the more symbolic and less verbal you can make your altar or spell artifacts, the better!

The issue of money comes down to two issues: greed and need.

Greed is by far the worst reason to work magic! Why? Magick has a price, think of it as a karmic price. A money spell by its very nature is driven by causes to manipulate a physical item. In essence, the money has to come from somewhere.

A lady I knew wished for half a million dollars. A few weeks later, she was involved in a serious industrial accident and the settlement was about half a million. She lost an arm and will never walk unassisted again. Was it worth the price?

A teenager I knew wished for a boatload of money. She received the money as the insurance beneficiary when her parents were killed in a car wreck.

On the other hand, a wish for bonafide need is something else altogether. A wish for the resources to deal with the financial situation is less invasive.

A lady I used to know wished for the resources to deal with the house she inherited from a recently deceased mother. A home I might add that required massive repair. The wish for the resources was not a wish for money. As it turned out, she was approached by a house flipper to fix up the residence, and both she and the house flipper made a tidy sum.

I knew a man who was concerned about a great deal of money he needed to send his kid to college; it was a costly school. He did a working for the resources to send his kid to university. As it turned out, two things happened: his kid changed his mind and decided to go to a much cheaper state school, and dad was promoted at work with a substantial raise in pay.

Never ask for the money. Instead, ask for the resources!

Love Spells

Love spells are messy, in my opinion. Even when done well, the results can be ambiguous.

There are factors to consider, one of them is **"time and season."** Are you really ready to receive that love of your life? A personal example: My spouse and I, forty years ago, would never have looked twice at each other, nor would we have given each other the time of day. Yet about 20 years ago, we, by chance, met at a party. Bam! Chemistry kicked in, and we became an item. We are each the love of the other's life. Neither of us can look at previous spouses and companions and say the same about them. Those people only helped season us into the people we are now.

If you aren't ready for the love of your life, no amount of having them underfoot now will make them right until you are both karmically ripe.

Case in point, I knew a very straight-laced lady, who, though she was up-and-coming in the legal profession, her life was empty for the "love of her life." Being a very talented magickal adept, she decided to take matters into her own hands and perform a spell working to bring the "love of her life" to her.

Her first mistake was serious consideration as to her specifications and filters in her ritual. The day came. She did her working on the right day, within the right planetary hours. It was as exacting a ceremony as you might expect from a perfectionist.

The first issue was that she considered herself a straight person and never thought of herself as gay. The second issue is that it wasn't her time and season. Perhaps it was karmic, no one knows for sure.

All these great men kept falling into her life, and not one of them resonated with her heart. She was in agony for nearly ten years. The only solace she had during all of this was a lady legal colleague whom she confided her deepest secrets and feelings. In the end, our heroine figured herself out, and the two women fell deeply in love and are now happily married.

Another adept of my acquaintance, a lady scientist who worked for a well-known government agency, was sick of not having a guy friend.

One day she did do a working to bring a great guy into her life. In the days following her working, she told another priestess and me what she had done. Of course, we both asked her what her filters were. *"I didn't put any filters on the guys; I figured I'd just wade through them."* I could only bite my lip in concern.

An hour later, after our downtown dinner, we all went to the local metro subway stop, our lovesick friend was going one way. My peer priestess and I went the other way. As it was Sunday, we all had a twenty-minute wait for our respective trains. During our wait, my friend and I watched in dismay as our lovesick friend was hit on by no less than twelve different guys. In the weeks that followed, she called me on the phone and lamented that it seemed that "every geek in DC was finding her."

Let me repeat this: Set Specifications and limits!

Weather Magick

Weather magick done well, and for the right intentions is terrific! Weather magick performed for ego or for reasonable comfort rarely turns out well.

For those reading this who do not believe in any of this magick, please feel free to move on to another chapter. For the practitioner, I must state for the record that I've seen some impressive weather work, good weather work, and sloppy weather work over the years. Finally, and sadly, I've seen my share of *"Oh my, what did you do?"*

I knew a little girl who was a natural weather adept. She could call in a snowstorm like the Army calls in an airstrike. These were mini-snowstorms that only seemed to affect the square mile or two around her parents' house; that in itself was truly eye-opening. Her parents, for years, logged all the school snow days she was responsible for. Please understand we are not talking about a snow flurry. No, we're talking about 6 to 12 inches of icy powder. In the few years that she ran in my witchy friendship circles, my nickname for her was the "Snow Queen."

One of my mentors, a Cherokee medicine guy, was a fantastic weather worker. In the late 1990s, I watched him punch a hole in a cloud cover. There was this hurricane off the mid-Atlantic coast. The cloud cover of the storm extended a few hundred miles from the eye which was out in the Atlantic. Several neighborhood children and I watched quietly as he chanted his prayers. All around the neighborhood, it was raining intensely except for the block where his house was. From where we were standing about 10 feet away from him, it was clear blue sky above.

Later in his house, we watched a recording of a local DC area 5 PM TV newscast. The weather guy was showing Doppler radar images of the cloud cover and pointed out the exception for this odd hole in the picture. I remember the weatherman remarking "That's interesting. Why is there a stationary clear spot over Silver Spring, Maryland?"

We all got a great laugh because we knew why. I learned my weather technique from Big Bear. I did not learn his Cherokee prayers. For the record, I must say the method is what this is about, not necessarily one man's prayers to the younger self for Weather relief.

About a year later, during an El Niño season, there was a severe rainstorm in the Washington DC area. The rain was coming down as if it was monsoon season. The monastics of the Buddhist monastery were preparing for a special kind of fire puja or fire-offering.

The problem was that the rain was coming down like someone had turned on a faucet. The monks in charge of the fire pit knew they could not start the fire in this sort of downpour.

An elder monastic knew of my skills and asked me to do something about the downpour. The request was simple: stop the deluge for 30 or 45 minutes so the monks could get a roaring fire going in the fire-offering pit. In essence, stop the rain so the people could pray and make offerings. That is a legitimate justification.

I agreed to help out. I took a small bowl of rice and a large Tibetan shell horn out into the yard in front of the Temple. I blew my horn and offered prayers in Tibetan and made offerings from a small bowl of rice and began blowing the horn again. About 10 minutes after my impromptu ritual, the rain diminished to a light sprinkle. Once again, this was reminiscent of Big Bear's working. Above the Temple and monastery grounds was a clear sky with stars above. About 45 minutes later, the fire was blazing. The clouds closed up over the temple grounds, and the rain started again. That was the successful part of the weather practice!

The lesson here is not to put loose conditions on your request prayer! Always set specifications!

Don't end the prayer by saying something like, "… And after the fire is bright and full, you can do as you wish…"

No, No, No, don't do this!

During our Buddhist ritual, there was rain, blowing wind, and the strangest lightning anyone had ever seen. Another Buddhist nun who was a witch as well leaned into me at one point and asked, "What did you do?"

The next day I got a phone call from Big Bear, and he asked simply if I've been working weather magick in the area of the Temple. Of course, I said yes.

He gave out a great belly laugh and remarked, "I have never seen purple and green lightning before… what did you do?"

Later that evening we had a long talk over supper about setting conditions with particular parameters in weather rituals. Frankly, I knew better, but I felt the words and technical advice from the elder and peer were constructive.

LESSON: Remember, no matter how old we are or how long we've been in the craft, we are always learning, and we are all still students of one degree or another.

Back to weather magick. A few weeks later, during that summer, the rain started again while we were at a Wicca camping event. Two younger students wanted a weather magick teaching, I agreed.

The rules for governing Weather magick are strict:

Weather magick can be done to:

- support the People's rituals,
- to protect the People,
- to relieve the People's suffering.

Stopping the rain for training or convenience doesn't fit into those rules. So, I decided the lesson had to be a gentle one, working within the boundaries of weather divas, not hard weather control magick.

I told the students each to grab a large baking bowl from camp supplies and to get soap and shampoo. Since we were all witches, nudity, wasn't an issue. We walked out into the rain and proceeded to soap up and effectively shower in the pouring rain. I told them to save shampooing for the last thing. By the time our bowls were full of rainwater, we had begun to shampoo. It was then, predictably, as our heads were full of shampoo, it stopped raining. With our bowls of water, we rinsed our hair. Obviously, the weather divas have a sense of humor!

Let's talk about another tradition.

Let's say you're Asian Buddhist, and you approached his holiness the Dalai Lama and explained that your home province was desperate for rain. He most likely would refer you to the high Lama in the Orthodox tradition of Tibetan Buddhism. The Dalai Lama is a member of the reformed tradition.

The Orthodox tradition has deep roots; 1000 years old in Tibet. The shamanic tradition was very much in flower. Then Padmasambhava came from India and taught the shamans Buddhist dharma and theory. The modern practitioners are called Ngak Phong.

In Tibetan culture, the Orthodox tradition has its roots in both shamanic magickal culture, and the tradition was the first to receive Buddhist thought. The shamans saw that Buddhist thought is totally compatible with their practices. Buddhism brought with it an ethical structure that helped discipline magickal practice. This doesn't mean that everyone who joins the modern Tibetan Orthodox tradition learns the art of magick. Absolutely not! But if you study Buddhist thought and you learn to read between the lines, you come to understand how delicate the fabric of reality is and how easy it is to manipulate it.

Remember: Reality is an illusion, and under the right conditions with the right mindset, the fabric of reality can be manipulated. This is what we teach in basic magickal practice.

When I embraced Buddhist thought, I found a home in the Tibetan Orthodox tradition. There are many adepts of the shamanic mindset within the Tibetan Orthodox tradition, and they are quite good at massaging the fabric of reality.

But I must caution those of you reading this book: do not run out and buy up all the books you can about Tibetan Buddhism. The things I have talked about regarding magick in that tradition require a greater understanding of what they are teaching.

The truth is you simply won't find a book that discusses practicing magick. What you will find is a comfortable place to understand Buddhist dharma and, on the side, classic metaphysics and a little bit of quantum theory. But it's never published in the clear! No, you must read between the lines and understand the fabric of reality.

One of the most famous Tibetan lamas, who was adept at weather magick, was the late Lama Yeshe Dorje. His revered nickname was the "Rain Maker."

A word of advice: if you think converting to Buddhism will lead to classes and instruction in Weather magick, I guarantee you it won't. It will, on the other hand, teach you to quiet the monkey chatter in your mind. Quieting the chatter in your psyche is a vital pre-requisite for such practices.

Part Six-The Art of Bread Making

Bread Making: A Path to Magickal Discipline

WHY? Practical Meditation Practice and Measurements and Process Discipline

Someday, you may want to work with potions and tinctures. You'll need the attention to detail, respect for process and patience that bread making will teach you. That's why!

I use bread as a teaching tool for several reasons. First, the bread is a great symbolic metaphor for the way magick is affected by good and sloppy practice. Second, making bread helps the practitioner relax and focus on something other than the self. Third, it's fun and you can eat it.

I'm strict on this notion: ***"If you can't make the bread; you'll never make the magick."***

Oh, I suppose, if you dabble long enough or take the dark path and use angry-hateful emotions to generate a manifestation you'll have some results. Results one shouldn't be proud of.

Look at it this way, if you have never baked before, I dare say if you attempted to bake a cake or make brownies from scratch, you'd probably fail. Most people do. I still haven't mastered either of them.

Baking is an acquired skill, so is magick.

Let's look at spells. Suppose you find an "old" book of magical spells in some used bookstore. In each of these spells is typically a list of odd substances or ingredients. Usually, these spell book recipes are accompanied by some incantation. Will it work?

I suppose it worked for the person who wrote the book. I doubt that it will work for you. First and foremost, old and even ancient spells and incantations are more or less useless to the modern practitioner, because the old symbols have little or no modern meaning to the contemporary adept.

But here's the problem. Let us suppose the book was written by some British witch. Right off the bat we have cultural issues with the ingredients. An herb ingredient in England might be called by a completely different name here in North America. Ingredients in themselves have no inherent magickal quality. These materials are in affect simply symbolic and are used to help the practitioner visualize some quality imagined in the substance.

At the core of magickal practice is visualization, and symbols are a very powerful way of visualizing.

So, our goal is to establish a common set of symbols amongst our student practitioners in order to teach the mechanics of magick. Once a student adept clearly understands the basic mechanics, then the symbology issue becomes easier.

We return to making a simple loaf of white bread. First, get the idea of making another type of bread, at least initially, out of your head. You have no idea how many of my witchlets cop an attitude, "oh I don't eat white sugar." or "I only eat whole wheat bread."

This exercise is not about what you'll eat, it's about whether you can master a basic loaf of white bread and that is all.

It never fails that a quarter of my students, on the first try at making simple white bread, decide to add other ingredients, because they obviously know better. Instead of white sugar they use brown sugar. Instead of plain ordinary flour they use whole wheat flour. Of course, my favorite, they toss some fruit like raisins into the bread. The results are always disastrous. You have no idea how hard it is for some people to stay on point and focus on the objective.

The objective is to not get fancy, but simply master a humble loaf of white bread. ONLY after the basic white loaf is mastered three times in a row do we move on to variations on the theme. As my track coach used to say, *"Keep running that play until you get it right."*

Mistakes are okay; rarely do people get it right the first time. Dealing with and accepting problems with the bread are an exercise in conquering your fat ego and taming it a bit. The best magick is performed with childlike innocence and humility. The basic bread making skill takes a little honing. If you keep each prep and baking consideration I teach you in the back of your mind, you'll master it.

Tools you'll need.

A kitchen thermometer
An oven thermometer
Liquid measuring vessel
Dry measure scoops
Measuring spoons
8 inch by 4 inch or metric equivalent metal bread pan

Ingredients

1 – Tablespoon of white sugar
1 – Package of dry yeast (2 ¼ teaspoons) DO NOT USE BREAD-MACHINE YEAST
1 ¼ cup of warm water. (100° to 112°)
3 cups of all-purpose flour
1/4 teaspoon of salt
Cooking Spray

Draw and mix warm and cold tap water, measure the temperature of the stream with your kitchen thermometer. When you have a stable 110°-112° for about 60 seconds, collect 1 ¼ cups of water from the tap stream. DO NOT MICROWAVE! (100° to 112°) No more than 115° otherwise you'll kill the yeast.

Mix your sugar and yeast into the water, set aside for about ten minutes. A foamy froth should appear on the top of the water. If not give it another 5 minutes. If the foamy froth doesn't appear the water was either too hot and you killed the yeast, or the yeast was old and not active. STOP

Rinse out the measuring cup and draw your warm water again, re-add your sugar and yeast and mix. Wait 10-15 minutes. If no foamy froth appears and if your water was spec at (100° to 112°) then go out and purchase some fresh yeast. Don't bother mixing it into the dry goods, it won't work and it's just a waste of materials. Go out and purchase some fresh yeast!

Let's assume you had a nice foamy froth on your water, sugar and yeast mixture.

Measure 3 cups of flour into a larger mixing bowl, stir in your ¼ teaspoon of salt.

Mix in your nice foamy froth water, sugar and yeast mixture. Stir with a large wooden or plastic spoon until a soft dough forms.

Sprinkle some flour on a large cutting board or a clean tabletop.

Wash your hands, dry and spray some cooking spray on your hands.

Remove the dough from the bowl and knead the dough until it becomes smooth with no chunks, and it becomes relatively elastic. Do no become too concerned if the dough it a bit dry at first. The kneading action will distribute the needed moisture evenly within the dough. If by chance it's a very dry, you can add water by sprinkling a few drops on the dough and working them in. NOTE: I said, a few drops!

After the first kneading, cover the bowl with a CLEAN damp towel and place in a warm place without drafts and allow the dough to rise for 30-45 minutes.

This is a good time to pre-heat your oven to 350°F. Use your OVEN thermometer to monitor the **real temperature** of the oven versus what the dial says. Most ovens are 25°-50°F off one way or another from the dial setting. Always use an oven thermometer to get it right! NEVER set the temperature and toss the bread into an oven coming up to temperature. You won't like the results. Pre-heat and once stable. Then and only then place the bread in the oven.

Added bonus: preheating oven helps make the room nice and warm to help the dough rise.

After the first rise, you will punch down the dough and allow it to rise again for perhaps 30 minutes. After the second rise, spray the bread pan with cooking spray; take the dough out roll and fold the dough into loaf roughly the size of the 8x4 bread pan. Place the dough in the bread pan. Optionally you can lightly spray a little cooking spray on the bread. Cover the bread pan and dough with that warm damp towel and allow the bread to rise.

After about another 20-30 minutes, the dough, set in a warm place, will rise to about double. Carefully remove the towel and place the bread pan in the oven. (I recommend that the warm place NOT be on top of the warm stove, the dough will get over heated!)

We bake for about 30-40 minutes at 350°F – typically about 35 minutes. Remember each loaf is different and each oven is different. This is a judgement call. At 30 minutes reach in and stick a long toothpick into the top of the bread, it comes back with dough sticking to it, give it more time. If it clean and the bread is browned to your liking remove and allow to cool.

After about 20-30 minutes – gently dump the bread out onto a clean kitchen towel and place on a wire cooling rack. After about an hour, feel free to slice off the end of the loaf. Look at the core of the bread; it is fully cooked or still doughy? If the bread is fully cooked, you got the time and temperature right.

If still doughy, give it 10-15 minutes more time the next time you make a loaf. **Rule:** do not adjust the temperature and the time together next time. Increase one or the other but not both. My experience suggests keeping the temperature stable and adding more time.

There, my witch friends, you have your **first spell** and your first magickal working. Bread is life! Eat and enjoy.

Remember: a magickal working requires the same attention to detail, fussing planning. If it was easy everyone would be doing it!

Failure Analysis

If the loaf failed, do a postmortem and examine every step you did.

Where you a cheap Charlie? Did you not purchase a kitchen or oven thermometer?

I bet you spent more money on a nice fancy wand or athame! The right tool for the right job! You can't guess these things; your hand is a horrible thermometer for water temperature testing.

Was the yeast too weak or too old? Was the water too hot or too cold?

Did you use whole wheat flour instead of all-purpose flour?

OH MY, did the dough overflow the bread pan and drip like stalagmites into the bottom of your oven? You didn't buy all-purpose flour, you probably purchased SELF-RISING flour. Wrong!

Was the bread in a drafty place during the rise? That's why it's a 2 inches/5cm thick in the bottom of the bread pan.

Was the oven at a stable temperature or still coming up to temperature?

Were you in a <u>hurry</u>? Did you toss the half-raised dough into a much hotter oven? Humm, that's why it's lopsided, cracking-upward and slanting off to one side.

DO NOT BE DEFEATED

BY A LITTLE LOAF OF WHITE BREAD!

You can do it, apply your intellect. Solve the problems! Read other books on the topic of bread making. Master it!

Closing Thoughts

The body of the essays in this book outlines a non-sectarian approach for practicing magick. I have been incredibly careful to frame all of it for the beginner and intermediate student of magick craft. That said, in the final analysis, we are all still students! I've been at it nearly 44 years as of this writing and there are still new things, I learn from reading the works of others and simply by experience.

Beginners to the magickal arts will find that by reading this book, they have an initial road map to practicing the mystical arts of Divining and Magickal manifestation. Of course, provided that they are willing to put in the work to learn to quiet their own minds.

More seasoned and advanced practitioners will no doubt read between the lines and glean some new perspective or some new tip.

I have explained the fundamental mechanics of divining and magickal practice in this book.

I have stated that I believe that basic magickal mechanics should be out there in plain language for everybody. Because in the end magick protects itself.

There are two types of magickal practitioners who can generate and execute effective magickal effect!

One group who accomplishes a mental quieting by using the traditional witchcraft stage props of robes, wands, crystals, incense, candles and carefully written rituals and spell verbiage meant to quiet the ordinary mind. All this effort is intended to instill within us a mood that it's now time to do magick. As well, if properly done, it generates rich mental imagery to pass along to the Younger self.

The other group doesn't use the traditional stage props but rather accomplishes a mental quieting by mastering the art of daily meditation to quiet-their-mind in order to project mental imagery to the younger self to execute effective magick or perform an act of divining!

You might ask which is better? They are both tried and truly effective methods for practicing the fine art of manifesting magick and accomplishing divining.

The approach and methods I have shared in this book are the lesser known and the aforementioned latter process for accomplishing mental quietness for practicing divining and for the purpose of magickal manifestation.

Please choose the path which best suits your lifestyle and mystical aspirations.

With deepest respects,

Cheryl "Lady Tashi" Costa 1/24/2022

About the Author

Mundane Life

Cheryl "Lady Tashi" Costa grew up in a small factory town in the northeast United States.

Cheryl is a veteran of two military services: Air Force with combat service in Vietnam; she also served in the Cold War Navy in Fast Attack Nuclear Submarines and later served in the Naval Reserve.

Professionally, Cheryl is a retired career Aerospace Industry Information Technology professional.

Vocationally, she's a published and produced playwright, an industrial film & indie film maker, a talk radio host, and a newspaper columnist.

Cheryl has a Bachelor of Arts degree from the State University of New York at Empire State College, in Entertainment Writing and Production.

Metaphysically

Maternal grandparents introduced her to the paranormal and instilled in Cheryl a sense of profound wonder concerning the mystical realm.

She was raised Roman Catholic and left that tradition at age 18.

She was introduced to Gardnerian Wicca in 1976 while in the Navy and became a solitary Wicca practitioner, and later in the 1980s she became a member of the Alexsanderian tradition. Lady Tashi's personal craft practices evolved as her experience grew. She has had many teachers and mystical mentors crossing the boundaries of numerous magickal and mystical traditions. She is initiated and ordained in numerous traditions. She served as a Tibetan Orthodox Buddhist monastic nun and is an ordained tantric Ngakma.

A witchcraft practitioner for most of her adult life, she has shared the gift of the magickal arts to many hundreds of students over forty plus years. After decades of magickal practice she considers herself a Mystic Witch. She retired as a Pastoral Priestess in December 2020.

The Media Witch

From 1991 through 1993, she produced the first regularly scheduled weekly cable program about American Witchcraft and Shamanism **KESTRYL AND COMPANY** on Channel 33 in Arlington, Virginia

Likewise, she has produced, been on-air talent and hosted numerous Talk Radio and Digital Radio program series.

WORKING GIRLS – WMET 1150AM Washington, DC 1994-1997

WORKING GIRLS RADIO – WWRC 570AM Washington, DC 1998

THE X FACTOR – WMET 1150AM Washington, DC 1998 - 2001

COSMIC QUESTIONS – KCOR digital radio, based in Las Vegas, Nevada 2018 - 2020

MYSTICAL MENTORS on Streaming - for ZYKOTIKA based in the United Kingdom 2022 - present

Cheryl (Lady Tashi) Costa, lives in quiet retreat with her wife in the regional Cleveland, Ohio area.

Lady Tashi is no longer taking on magickal students.

But if you've read this book, you are welcome to correspond with her via EMAIL: **cherylcosta.mystic@gmail.com**

Made in the USA
Las Vegas, NV
03 October 2023

78516068R00081